LONDON CRITICS

greeted *Luther* as Osborne's finest achievement and his most substantial contribution as a major dramatist. Departing from the manner of his earlier works, which electrified audiences with their ruthless, idiomatic observations on contemporary life, Osborne attains an epic, formal grandeur in *Luther.*

Osborne portrays the fierce and grappling spirit of a defiant priest, in a language that soars to the heights of dramatic poetry. His portrait of Luther is so intimate as to be unnerving to the viewer; so passionate that it succeeds in echoing the lonely anguish of every rebel in every age. . . .

". . . full of argument and invective. Scene after scene comes alive when ideas are thrown from hand-to-hand like grenades."
Alan Brien, The London Sunday Telegraph

LUTHER

A PLAY BY

John Osborne

A SIGNET BOOK

NEW AMERICAN LIBRARY

SIGNET TRADEMARK REG. U.S. PAT. OFF. AND FOREIGN COUNTRIES
REGISTERED TRADEMARK—MARCA REGISTRADA
HECHO EN CHICAGO, U.S.A.

SIGNET, SIGNET CLASSIC, MENTOR, PLUME, MERIDIAN AND NAL BOOKS *are published by New American Library, 1633 Broadway, New York, New York 10019*

FIRST SIGNET PRINTING, OCTOBER, 1963

11   12   13   14   15   16   17   18   19

PRINTED IN THE UNITED STATES OF AMERICA

The first performance of LUTHER was given at the Theatre Royal, Nottingham, on June 26th, 1961, by the English Stage Company. It was directed by Tony Richardson and the décor was by Jocelyn Herbert. The part of Luther was played by Albert Finney.

CAST

KNIGHT

PRIOR

MARTIN

HANS

LUCAS

WEINAND

TETZEL

STAUPITZ

CAJETAN

MILTITZ

LEO

ECK

KATHERINE

HANS, THE YOUNGER

AUGUSTINIANS, DOMINICANS,
HERALD, EMPEROR, PEASANTS, ETC.

My dear boy, are you all right? You're so pal

ACT ONE

Scene 1. The convent of the Augustinian Order of
Eremites at Erfurt. 1506

Scene 2. The same. A year later

Scene 3. Two hours later

ACT TWO

Scene 1. The market place. Jüterbog. 1517

Scene 2. The Eremite Cloister. Wittenberg. 1517

Scene 3. The steps of the Castle Church. Wittenberg.
Eve of All Saints. 1517

Scene 4. The Fugger Palace. Augsburg. October 1518

Scene 5. A hunting lodge. Magliana, Italy. 1519

Scene 6. The Elster Gate. Wittenberg. 1520

ACT THREE

Scene 1. The Diet of Worms. 1521

Scene 2. Wittenberg. 1525

Scene 3. The Eremite Cloister. Wittenberg. 1530.

NOTE

*At the opening of each act, the Knight appears. He
grasps a banner and briefly barks the time and place
of the scene following at the audience, and then retires.*

ACT ONE

Scene One

*The Cloister Chapel of the Eremites of St. Augustine.
Erfurt, Thuringia, 1506.* MARTIN *is being received into
the Order. He is kneeling in front of the* PRIOR *in the
presence of the assembled convent.*

PRIOR:
Now you must choose one of two ways: either to leave
us now, or give up this world, and consecrate and de-
vote yourself entirely to God and our Order. But I must
add this: once you have committed yourself, you are not
free, for whatever reason, to throw off the yoke of obedience, for you will have accepted it freely, while you
were still able to discard it.

> (*The habit and hood of the Order are brought in
> and blessed by the* PRIOR.)

PRIOR:
He whom it was your will to dress in the garb of the
Order, oh Lord, invest him also with eternal life.

> (*He undresses* MARTIN.)

PRIOR:
The Lord divest you of the former man and of all his
works. The Lord invest you with the new man.

> (*The* CHOIR *sings as* MARTIN *is robed in the habit
> and hood. The long white scapular is thrown over
> his head and hung down, before and behind; then
> he kneels again before the* PRIOR, *and, with his hand
> on the statutes of the Order, swears the oath.*)

MARTIN:
I, brother Martin, do make profession and promise obe-

dience to Almighty God, to Mary the Sacred Virgin, and
to you, my brother Prior of this cloister, in the name of
the Vicar General of the order of Eremites of the holy
Bishop of St. Augustine and his successors, to live without property and in chastity according to the Rule of our
Venerable Father Augustine until death.

> (*The* PRIOR *wishes a prayer over him, and* MARTIN
> *prostrates himself with arms extended in the form
> of a cross.*)

PRIOR:
Lord Jesus Christ, our leader and our strength, by the
fire of humility you have set aside this servant, Martin,
from the rest of Mankind. We humbly pray that this fire
will also cut him off from carnal intercourse and
from the community of those things done on earth by
men, through the sanctity shed from heaven upon him,
and that you will bestow on him grace to remain yours,
and merit eternal life. For it is not he who begins, but
he who endures will be saved. Amen.

> (*The* CHOIR *sings Veni Creator Spiritus or per-
> haps Great Father Augustine*). *A newly lighted taper
> is put into* MARTIN'S *hands, and he is led up the
> altar steps to be welcomed by the monks with the
> kiss of peace. Then, in their midst, he marches slowly
> with them behind the screen and is lost to sight.
> The procession disappears, and, as the sound of
> voices dies away, two men are left alone in the
> congregation. One of them,* HANS, *gets up impatient-
> ly and moves down-stage. It is* MARTIN'S FATHER,
> *a stocky man wired throughout with a miner's mus-
> cle, lower-middle class, on his way to become a
> small, primitive capitalist; bewildered, full of pride
> and resentment. His companion,* LUCAS, *finishes a
> a respectful prayer and joins him.*)

HANS:
Well?

LUCAS:
Well?

HANS:
Don't 'well' me, you feeble old ninny, what do you think?

LUCAS:
Think? Of what?

HANS:
Yes, think man, think, what do you think, pen and ink, think of all that?

LUCAS:
Oh—

HANS:
Oh! Of all these monks, of Martin and all the rest of it, what do you think? You've been sitting in this arse-aching congregation all this time, you've been watching, haven't you? What about it?

LUCAS:
Yes, well, I must say it's all **very impressive.**

HANS:
Oh, yes?

LUCAS:
No getting away from it.

HANS:
Impressive?

LUCAS:
Deeply. It was moving and oh——

HANS:
What?

LUCAS:
You must have felt it, surely. You couldn't fail to.

HANS:
Impressive! I don't know what impresses me any longer.

LUCAS:
Oh, come on———

HANS:
Impressive!

LUCAS:
Of course it is, and you know it.

HANS:
Oh, you—you can afford to be impressed.

LUCAS:
It's surely too late for any regrets, or bitterness, Hans.
It obviously must be God's will, and there's an end of it.

HANS:
That's exactly what it is—an end of it! Very fine for you,
my old friend, very fine indeed. You're just losing a son-
in-law, and you can take your pick of plenty more of
those where he comes from. But what am I losing? I'm
losing a son; mark: a son.

LUCAS:
How can you say that?

HANS:
How can I say it? I do say it, that's how. Two sons to the
plague, and now another. God's eyes! Did you see that
haircut? Brother Martin!

LUCAS:
There isn't a finer order than these people, not the
Dominicans or Franciscans———

HANS:
Like an egg with a beard.

LUCAS:
You said that yourself.

HANS:
Oh, I suppose they're Christians under their damned
cowls.

LUCAS:
There are good, distinguished men in this place, and well
you know it.

HANS:
Yes—good, distinguished men——

LUCAS:
Pious, learned men, men from the University like Martin.

HANS:
Learned men! Some of them can't read their own names.

LUCAS:
So?

HANS:
So! I—I'm a miner. I don't need books. You can't see
to read books under the ground. But Martin's a scholar.

LUCAS:
He most certainly is.

HANS:
A Master of Arts! What's he master of now? Eh? Tell me.

LUCAS:
Well, there it is. God's gain is your loss.

HANS:
Half these monks do nothing but wash dishes and beg in
the streets.

LUCAS:
We should be going, I suppose.

HANS:
He could have been a man of stature.

LUCAS:
And he will, with God's help.

HANS:
Don't tell me. He could have been a lawyer.

LUCAS:
Well, he won't now.

HANS:
No, you're damn right he won't. Of stature. To the Archbishop, or the Duke, or——

LUCAS:
Yes.

HANS:
Anyone.

LUCAS:
Come on.

HANS:
Anyone you can think of.

LUCAS:
Well, I'm going.

HANS:
Brother Martin!

LUCAS:
Hans.

HANS:

Do you know why? Lucas: Why? What made him do it?
(*He has ceased to play a role by this time and he
asks the question simply as if he expected a short,
direct answer.*)

HANS:

What made him do it?
(LUCAS *grasps his forearm.*)

LUCAS:

Let's go home.

HANS:

Why? That's what I can't understand. Why? Why?

LUCAS:

Home. Let's go home.
(*They go off. The convent bell rings. Some monks
are standing at a refectory table. After their prayers, they sit down, and, as they eat in silence, one
of the Brothers reads from a lectern. During this
short scene,* MARTIN, *wearing a rough apron over
his habit, waits on the others.*)

READER:

What are the tools of Good Works?
First, to love Lord God with all one's heart, all one's
soul, and all one's strength. Then, one's neighbour as
oneself. Then, not to kill.
Not to commit adultery
Not to steal
Not to covet
Not to bear false witness
To honour all men
To deny yourself, in order to follow Christ
To chastise the body
Not to seek soft living
To love fasting
To clothe the naked
To visit the sick

To bury the dead
To help the afflicted
To console the sorrowing
To prefer nothing to the love of Christ

Not to yield to anger
Not to nurse a grudge
Not to hold guile in your heart
Not to make a feigned peace
To fear the Day of Judgment
To dread Hell
To desire eternal life with all your spiritual longing
To keep death daily before your eyes
To keep constant vigilance over the actions of your life
To know for certain that God sees you everywhere
When evil thoughts come into your heart, to dash them
at once on the love of Christ and to manifest them to
your spiritual father
To keep your mouth from evil and depraved talk
Not to love much speaking
Not to speak vain words or such as produce laughter
To listen gladly to holy readings
To apply yourself frequently to prayer
Daily in your prayer, with tears and sighs to confess your
past sins to God
Not to fulfil the desires of the flesh
To hate your own will

Behold, these are the tools of the spiritual craft. If we
employ these unceasingly day and night, and render account of them on the Day of Judgment, then we shall receive from the Lord in return that reward that He Himself has promised: Eye hath not seen nor ear heard what
God hath prepared for those that love him. Now this is
the workshop in which we shall diligently execute all
these tasks. May God grant that you observe all these
rules cheerfully as lovers of spiritual beauty, spreading
around you by the piety of your deportment the sweet
odour of Christ.

(The convent bell rings. The MONKS *rise, bow their
heads in prayer, and then move upstage to the*

steps where they kneel. MARTIN, *assisted by another
Brother, stacks the table and clears it. Presently,
they all prostrate themselves, and, beneath flaming
candles, a communal confession begins.* MARTIN *returns and prostrates himself downstage behind the
rest. This scene throughout is urgent, muted, almost
whispered, confidential, secret, like a prayer.*)

BROTHER:

I confess to God, to Blessed Mary and our holy Father
Augustine, to all the saints, and to all present that I have
sinned exceedingly in thought, word and deed by my own
fault. Wherefore I pray Holy Mary, all the saints of God
and you all assembled here to pray for me. I confess I
did leave my cell for the Night Office without the
Scapular and had to return for it. Which is a deadly in-
fringement of the first degree of humility, that of obedience without delay. For this failure to Christ I abjectly
seek forgiveness and whatever punishment the Prior and
community is pleased to impose on me.

MARTIN:

I am a worm and no man, a byword and a laughing
stock. Crush out the worminess in me, stamp on me.

BROTHER:

I confess I have three times made mistakes in the Ora-
tory, in psalm singing and Antiphon.

MARTIN:

I was fighting a bear in a garden without flowers, leading
into a desert. His claws kept making my arms bleed as I
tried to open a gate which would take me out. But the
gate was no gate at all. It was simply an open frame, and
I could have walked through it, but I was covered in my
own blood, and I saw a naked woman riding on a goat,
and the goat began to drink my blood, and I thought I
should faint with the pain and I awoke in my cell, all
soaking in the devil's bath.

BROTHER:

Let Brother Norbert remember also his breakage while working in the kitchen.

BROTHER:

I remember it, and confess humbly.

BROTHER:

Let him remember also his greater transgression in not coming at once to the Prior and community to do penance for it, and so increasing his offence.

MARTIN:

I am alone. I am alone, and against myself.

BROTHER:

I confess it. I confess it, and beg your prayers that I may undergo the greater punishment for it.

MARTIN:

How can I justify myself?

BROTHER:

Take heart, you shall be punished, and severely.

MARTIN:

How can I be justified?

BROTHER:

I confess I have failed to rise from my bed speedily enough. I arrived at the Night Office after the Gloria of the 94th Psalm, and though I seemed to amend the shame by not standing in my proper place in the choir, and standing in the place appointed by the Prior for such careless sinners so that they may be seen by all, my fault is too great and I seek punishment.

MARTIN:

I was among a group of people, men and women, fully clothed. We lay on top of each other in neat rows about seven or eight across. Eventually, the pile was many peo-

ple deep. Suddenly, I panicked—although I was on top
of the pile—and I cried: what about those underneath?
Those at the very bottom, and those in between? We all
got up in an orderly way, without haste, and when we
looked, those at the bottom were not simply flattened
by the weight, they were just their clothes, they were just
their clothes, neatly pressed and folded on the ground.
They were their clothes, neatly pressed and folded on
the ground.

BROTHER:
I did omit to have a candle ready at the Mass.

BROTHER:
Twice in my sloth, I have omitted to shave, and even ex-
cused myself, pretending to believe my skin to be fairer
than that of my Brothers, and my beard lighter and my
burden also. I have been vain and slothful, and I beg
forgiveness and ask penance.

MARTIN:
If my flesh would leak and dissolve, and I could live as
bone, if I were forged bone, plucked bone and brain,
warm hair and a bony heart, if I were all bone, I could
brandish myself without terror, without any terror at all
—I could be indestructible.

BROTHER:
I did ask for a bath, pretending to myself that it was
necessary for my health, but as I lowered my body into
the tub, it came to me that it was inordinate desire and
that it was my soul that was soiled.

MARTIN:
My bones fail. My bones fail, my bones are shattered
and fall away, my bones fail and all that's left of me is a
scraped marrow and a dying jelly.

BROTHER:
Let Brother Paulinus remember our visit to our near

sister house, and lifting his eyes repeatedly at a woman in the town who dropped alms into his bag.

BROTHER:
I remember, and I beg forgiveness.

BROTHER:
Then let him remember also that though our dear Father Augustine does not forbid us to see women, he blames us if we should desire them or wish to be the object of their desire. For it is not only by touch and by being affectionate that a man excites disorderly affection in a woman. This can be done also even by looks. You cannot maintain that your mind is pure if you have *wanton* eyes. For a wanton eye is a wanton heart. When people with impure hearts manifest their inclination towards each other through the medium of looks, even though no word is spoken, and when they take pleasure in their desire for each other, the purity of their character has gone even though they may be undefiled by any unchaste act. He who fixes his eyes on a woman and takes pleasure in her glance, must not think that he goes unobserved by his brothers.

MARTIN:
I confess that I have offended grievously against humility, being sometimes discontented with the meanest and worst of everything, I have not only failed to declare myself to myself lower and lower and of less account than all other men, but I have failed in my most inmost heart to believe it. For many weeks, many weeks it seemed to me, I was put to cleaning the latrines. I did it, and I did it vigorously, not tepidly, with all my poor strength, without whispering or objections to anyone. But although I fulfilled my task, and I did it well, sometimes there were murmurings in my heart. I prayed that it would cease, knowing that God, seeing my murmuring heart, must reject my work, and it was as good as not done. I sought out my master, and he punished me, telling me to fast for two days. I have fasted for three, but, even so, I can't tell if the murmurings are really gone,

and I ask for your prayers, and I ask for your prayers
that I may be able to go on fulfilling the same task.

BROTHER:
Let Brother Martin remember all the degrees of humility;
and let him go on cleaning the latrines.

> (*The convent bell rings. After lying prostrate for a
> few moments, all the* BROTHERS, *including* MARTIN,
> *rise and move to the* CHOIR. *The office begins,
> versicle, antiphon and psalm, and* MARTIN *is lost to
> sight in the ranks of his fellow* MONKS. *Presently,
> there is a quiet, violent moaning, just distinguish-
> able amongst the voices. It becomes louder and
> wilder, the cries more violent, and there is some
> confusion in* MARTIN'S *section of the* CHOIR. *The sing-
> ing goes on with only a few heads turned. It seems
> as though the disturbance has subsided.* MARTIN *ap-
> pears, and staggers between the stalls. Outstretched
> hands fail to restrain him, and he is visible to all,
> muscles rigid, breath suspended, then jerking un-
> controllably as he is seized in a raging fit. Two*
> BROTHERS *go to him, but* MARTIN *writhes with such
> ferocity, that they can scarcely hold him down. He
> tries to speak, the effort is frantic, and eventually,
> he is able to roar out a word at a time.*)

MARTIN:
Not! Me! I am *not!*

> (*The attack reaches its height, and he recoils as if
> he had bitten his tongue and his mouth were full of
> blood and saliva. Two more* MONKS *come to help,
> and he almost breaks away from them, but the ef-
> fort collapses, and they are able to drag him away,
> as he is about to vomit. The Office continues as if
> nothing had taken place.*)

(*End of Act One—Scene One*)

ACT ONE

SCENE TWO

A knife, like a butcher's, hanging aloft, the size of a garden fence. The cutting edge of the blade points upwards. Across it hangs the torso of a naked man, his head hanging down. Below it, an enormous round cone, like the inside of a vast barrel, surrounded by darkness. From the upstage entrance, seemingly far, far away, a dark figure appears against the blinding light inside, as it grows brighter. The figure approaches slowly along the floor of the vast cone, and stops as it reaches the downstage opening. It is MARTIN, *haggard and streaming with sweat.*

MARTIN:
I lost the body of a child, a child's body, the eyes of a child; and at the first sound of my own childish voice. I lost the body of a child; and I was afraid, and I went back to find it. But I'm still afraid. I'm afraid, and there's an end of it! But *I* mean . . . (*shouts*) . . . Continually! For instance of the noise the Prior's dog makes on a still evening when he rolls over on his side and licks his teeth. I'm afraid of the darkness, and the hole in it; and I see it sometime of every day! And some days more than once even, and there's no bottom to it, no bottom to my breath, and I can't reach it. Why? Why do you think? There's a bare fist clenched to my bowels and they can't move, and I have to sit sweating in my little monk's house to open them. The lost body of a child, hanging on a mother's tit, and close to the warm, big body of a man, and I can't find it.
(*He steps down, out of the blazing light within the cone, and goes to his cell down* L. *Kneeling by his bed, he starts to try and pray but he soon collapses. From down* R *appear a procession of* MONKS,

24

*carrying various priest's vestments, candles and ar-
ticles for the altar, for* MARTIN *is about to perform
his very first Mass. Heading them is* BROTHER
WEINAND. *They pass* MARTIN'S *cell, and, after a few
words, they go on, leaving* BROTHER WEINAND *with
,MARTIN, and disappear into what is almost like a
small house on the upstage left of the stage: a bagpipe of the period, fat, soft, foolish and obscene
looking.)*

BRO. WEINAND:
Brother Martin! Brother Martin!

MARTIN:
Yes.

BRO. WEINAND:
Your father's here.

MARTIN:
My father?

BRO. WEINAND:
He asked to see you, but I told him it'd be better to
wait until afterwards.

MARTIN:
Where is he?

BRO. WEINAND:
He's having breakfast with the Prior.

MARTIN:
Is he alone?

BRO. WEINAND:
No, he's got a couple of dozen friends at least, I should
say.

MARTIN:
Is my mother with him?

BRO. WEINAND:
No.

MARTIN:
What did he have to come for? I should have told him
not to come.

BRO. WEINAND:
It'd be a strange father who didn't want to be present
when his son celebrated his first Mass.

MARTIN:
I never thought he'd come. Why didn't he tell me?

BRO. WEINAND:
Well, he's here now, anyway. He's also given twenty
guilden to the chapter as a present, so he can't be too
displeased with you.

MARTIN:
Twenty guilden.

BRO. WEINAND:
Well, are you all prepared?

MARTIN:
That's three times what it cost him to send me to the
University for a year.

BRO. WEINAND:
You don't look it. Why, you're running all over with
sweat again. Are you sick? Are you?

MARTIN:
No.

BRO. WEINAND:
Here, let me wipe your face. You haven't much time.
You're sure you're not sick?

MARTIN:
My bowels won't move, that's all. But that's nothing out of the way.

BRO. WEINAND:
Have you shaved?

MARTIN:
Yes. Before I went to confession. Why, do you think I should shave again?

BRO. WEINAND:
No. I don't. A few overlooked little bristles couldn't make much difference, any more than a few imaginary sins. There, that's better.

MARTIN:
What do you mean?

BRO. WEINAND:
You were sweating like a pig in a butcher's shop. You know what they say, don't you? Wherever you find a melancholy person, there you'll find a bath running for the devil.

MARTIN:
No, no, what did you mean about leaving a few imaginary sins?

BRO. WEINAND:
I mean there are plenty of priests with dirty ears administering the sacraments, but this isn't the time to talk about that. Come on, Martin, you've got nothing to be afraid of.

MARTIN:
How do you know?

BRO. WEINAND:
You always talk as if lightning were just about to strike behind you.

MARTIN:
Tell me what you meant.

BRO. WEINAND:
I only meant the whole convent knows you're always making up sins you've never committed. That's right— well, isn't it? No sensible confessor will have anything to do with you.

MARTIN:
What's the use of all this talk of penitence if I can't feel it.

BRO. WEINAND:
Father Nathin told me he had to punish you only the day before yesterday because you were in some ridiculous state of hysteria, all over some verse in Proverbs or something.

MARTIN:
"Know thou the state of thy flocks."

BRO. WEINAND:
And all over the interpretation of one word apparently. When will you ever learn? You must know what you're doing. Some of the brothers laugh quite openly at you, you and your over-stimulated conscience. Which is wrong of them, I know, but you must be able to see why.

MARTIN:
It's the single words that trouble me.

BRO. WEINAND:
The moment you've confessed and turned to the altar, you're beckoning for a priest again. Why, every time you break wind they say you rush to a confessor.

MARTIN:
Do they say that?

BRO. WEINAND:
It's their favourite joke.

MARTIN:
They say that, do they?

BRO. WEINAND:
Martin! You're protected from many of the world's evils
in here. You're expected to master them, not be obsessed by them. God bids us hope in His everlasting
mercy. Try to remember that.

MARTIN:
And you tell me this! What have I gained from coming
into this sacred Order? Aren't I still the same? I'm still
envious, I'm still impatient, I'm still passionate?

BRO. WEINAND:
How can you ask a question like that?

MARTIN:
I do ask it. I'm asking you! What have I gained?

BRO. WEINAND:
In any of this, all we can ever learn is how to die.

MARTIN:
That's no answer.

BRO. WEINAND:
It's the only one I can think of at this moment. Come on.

MARTIN:
All you teach me in this sacred place is how to doubt——

BRO. WEINAND:
Give you a little praise, and you're pleased for a while,
but let a little trial of sin and death come into your day
and you crumble, don't you?

MARTIN:
But that's all you've taught me, that's really all you've
taught me, and all the while I'm living in the Devil's
worm-bag.

BRO. WEINAND:
It hurts me to watch you like this, sucking up cares like a leech.

MARTIN:
You *will* be there beside me, won't you?

BRO. WEINAND:
Of course, and, if anything at all goes wrong, or if you forget anything, we'll see to it. You'll be all right. But nothing will—you won't make any mistakes.

MARTIN:
But what if I do, just one mistake. Just a word, one word—one sin.

BRO. WEINAND:
Martin, kneel down.

MARTIN:
Forgive me, Brother Weinand, but the truth is this——

BRO. WEINAND:
Kneel.
        (MARTIN *kneels.*)

MARTIN:
It's this, just this. All I can feel, all I can feel is God's hatred.

BRO. WEINAND:
Repeat the Apostles' Creed.

MARTIN:
He's like a glutton, the way he gorges me, he's a glutton. He gorges me, and then spits me out in lumps.

BRO. WEINAND:
After me. "I believe in God the Father Almighty, maker of Heaven and Earth . . .

MARTIN:
I'm a trough, I tell you, and he's swilling about in me.
All the time.

BRO. WEINAND:
"And in Jesus Christ, His only Son Our Lord . . .

MARTIN:
"And in Jesus Christ, His only Son Our Lord . . .

BRO. WEINAND:
"Who was conceived by the Holy Ghost, born of the
Virgin Mary, suffered under Pontius Pilate . . .

MARTIN (*almost unintelligibly*):
"Was crucified, dead and buried; He descended into
Hell; the third day He rose from the dead, He ascended
into Heaven, and sitteth on the right hand of God the
Father Almighty; from thence He shall come to judge
the quick and the dead." And every sunrise sings a song
for death.

BRO. WEINAND:
"I believe——

MARTIN:
"I believe——

BRO. WEINAND:
Go on.

MARTIN:
"I believe in the Holy Ghost; the holy Catholic Church;
the Communion of Saints; the forgiveness of sins;

BRO. WEINAND:
Again!

MARTIN:
"The forgiveness of sins.

BRO. WEINAND:
What was that again?

MARTIN:
"I believe in the forgiveness of sins."

BRO. WEINAND:
Do you? Then remember this: St. Bernard says that
when we say in the Apostles' Creed "I believe in the
forgiveness of sins" each one must believe that *his* sins
are forgiven. Well?——

MARTIN:
I wish my bowels would open. I'm blocked up like an old
crypt.

BRO. WEINAND:
Try to remember, Martin?

MARTIN:
Yes, I'll try.

BRO. WEINAND:
Good. Now, you must get yourself ready. Come on, we'd
better help you.
> (*Some* BROTHERS *appear from out of the bagpipe
> with the vestments, etc. and help* MARTIN *put them
> on.*)

MARTIN:
How much did you say my father gave to the chapter?

BRO. WEINAND:
Twenty guilden.

MARTIN:
That's a lot of money to my father. He's a miner, you
know.

BRO. WEINAND:
Yes, he told me.

MARTIN:
As tough as you can think of. Where's he sitting?

BRO. WEINAND:
Near the front, I should think. Are you nearly ready?
  (*The Convent bell rings. A procession leads out
  from the bagpipe.*)

MARTIN:
Thank you, Brother Weinand.

BRO. WEINAND:
For what? Today would be an ordeal for any kind of
man. In a short while, you will be handling, for the first
time, the body and blood of Christ. God bless you, my
son.
  (*He makes the sign of the cross, and the other
  BROTHERS leave.*)

MARTIN:
Somewhere, in the body of a child, Satan foresaw in me
what I'm suffering now. That's why he prepares open pits
for me, and all kinds of tricks to bring me down, so that
I keep wondering if I'm the only man living who's baited,
and surrounded by dreams, and afraid to move.

BRO. WEINAND (*really angry by now*):
You're a fool. You're really a fool. God isn't angry with
you. It's you who are angry with Him.
  (*He goes out. The BROTHERS wait for MARTIN, who
  kneels.*)

MARTIN:
Oh, Mary, dear Mary, all I see of Christ is a flame and
raging on a rainbow. Pray to your Son, and ask Him to
still His anger, for I can't raise my eyes to look at Him.
Am I the only one to see all this, and suffer?
  (*He rises, joins the procession and disappears off
  with it.
  As the Mass is heard to begin offstage, the stage
  is empty. Then the light within the cone grows in-*

creasingly brilliant, and, presently MARTIN *appears
again. He enters through the far entrance of the
cone, and advances towards the audience. He is
carrying a naked child. Presently, he steps down
from the cone, comes downstage, and stands still.*)

MARTIN:
And so, the praising ended—and the blasphemy began.
(*He returns, back into the cone, the light fades as
the Mass comes to its end.*)

(*End of Act One—Scene Two*)

ACT ONE

Scene Three

The Convent refectory. Some monks are sitting at table with HANS *and* LUCAS. LUCAS *is chatting with the* BROTHERS *eagerly, but* HANS *is brooding. He has drunk a lot of wine in a short time, and his brain is beginning to heat.*

HANS:
What about some more of this, eh? Don't think you can get away with it, you know, you old cockchafer. I'm getting me twenty guilden's worth before the day's out. After all, it's a proud day for all of us. That's right, isn't it?

LUCAS:
It certainly is.

BRO. WEINAND:
Forgive me, I wasn't looking. Here——
    (*He fills* HANS'S *glass.*)

HANS (*trying to be friendly*):
Don't give me that. You monks don't miss much. Got eyes like gimlets and ears like open drains. Tell me— Come on, then, what's your opinion of Brother Martin?

BRO. WEINAND:
He's a good, devout monk.

HANS:
Yes. Yes, well, I suppose you can't say much about each other, can you? You're more like a team, in a way. Tell me, Brother—would you say that in this monastery—or,

any monastery you like—you were as strong as the weakest member of the team?

BRO. WEINAND:
No, I don't think that's so.

HANS:
But wouldn't you say then—I'm not saying this in any criticism, mind, but because I'm just interested, naturally, in the circumstances—but wouldn't you say that one bad monk, say for instance, one really monster sized, roaring great bitch of a monk, if he really got going, really going, couldn't he get his order such a reputation that eventually, it might even have to go into—what do they call it now—liquidation. That's it. Liquidation. Now, you're an educated man, you understand Latin and Greek and Hebrew——

BRO. WEINAND:
Only Latin, I'm afraid, and a very little Greek.

HANS (*having planted his cue for a quick, innocent boast*):
Oh, really. Martin knows Latin and Greek, and now he's half-way through Hebrew too, they tell me.

BRO. WEINAND:
Martin is a brilliant man. We are not all as gifted as he is.

HANS:
No, well, anyway what would be your opinion about this?

BRO. WEINAND:
I think my opinion would be that the Church is bigger than those who are in her.

HANS:
Yes, yes, but don't you think it could be discredited by, say, just a few men?

BRO. WEINAND:
Plenty of people have tried, but the Church is still there.
Besides, a human voice is small and the world's very
large. But the Church reaches out and is heard everywhere.

HANS:
Well, what about this chap Erasmus, for instance?

BRO. WEINAND (*politely. He knows* HANS *knows nothing
about him*):
Yes?

HANS:
Erasmus. (*Trying to pass the ball*). Well, what about
him, for instance? What do you think about him?

BRO. WEINAND:
Erasmus is apparently a great scholar, and respected
throughout Europe.

HANS (*resenting being lectured*):
Yes, of course, *I* know who he is, I don't need you to tell
me that, what I said was: what do you think about him?

BRO. WEINAND:
Think about him?

HANS:
Good God, you won't stand still a minute and let yourself be saddled, will you? Doesn't he criticize the Church
or something?

BRO. WEINAND:
He's a scholar, and, I should say, his criticisms could
only be profitably argued about by other scholars.

LUCAS:
Don't let him get you into an argument. He'll argue about
anything, especially if he doesn't know what he's talking
about.

HANS:
I know what I'm talking about, I was merely asking a question——

LUCAS:
Well, you shouldn't be asking questions on a day like today. Just think of it, for a minute, Hans——

HANS:
What do you think I'm doing? You soppy old woman!

LUCAS:
It's a really 'once only' occasion, like a wedding, if you like.

HANS:
Or a funeral. By the way, what's happened to the corpse? Eh? Where's Brother Martin?

BRO. WEINAND:
I expect he's still in his cell.

HANS:
Well, what's he doing in there?

BRO. WEINAND:
He's perfectly all right, he's a little—disturbed.

HANS (*pouncing delightedly*):
Disturbed! Disturbed! What's he disturbed about?

BRO. WEINAND:
Celebrating one's first Mass can be a great ordeal for a sensitive spirit.

HANS:
Oh, the bread and the wine and all that?

BRO. WEINAND:
Of course; there are a great many things to memorize as well.

LUCAS:
Heavens, yes. I don't know how they think of it all.

HANS:
I didn't think he made it up as he went along! But doesn't he know we're still here? Hasn't anybody told him we're all waiting for him?

BRO. WEINAND:
He won't be much longer—you'll see. Here, have some more of our wine. He simply wanted to be on his own for a little while before he saw anyone.

HANS:
I should have thought he had enough of being on his own by now.

LUCAS:
The boy's probably a bit—well, you know, anxious about seeing you again too.

HANS:
What's he got to be anxious about?

LUCAS:
Well, apart from anything else, it's nearly three years since he last saw you.

HANS:
I saw *him*. He didn't see me.
    (*Enter* MARTIN.)

LUCAS:
There you are, my boy. We were wondering what had happened to you. Come and sit down, there's a good lad. Your father and I have been punishing the convent wine cellar, I'm afraid. Bit early in the day for me, too.

HANS:
Speak for yourself, you swirly-eyed old gander. We're not *started* yet, are we?

LUCAS:
My dear boy, are you all right? You're so pale.

HANS:
He's right though. Brother Martin! Brother Lazarus they ought to call you!
> (*He laughs and* MARTIN *smiles at the joke with him.* MARTIN *is cautious,* HANS *too, but manœuvring for position.*)

MARTIN:
I'm all right, thank you, Lucas.

HANS:
Been sick, have you?

MARTIN:
I'm much better now, thank you, father.

HANS (*relentless*):
Upset tummy, is it? That what it is? Too much fasting I expect. (*Concealing concern*). You look like death warmed up, all right.

LUCAS:
Come and have a little wine. You're allowed that, aren't you? It'll make you feel better.

HANS:
I know that milky look. I've seen it too many times. Been sick have you?

LUCAS:
Oh, he's looking better already. Drop of wine'll put the colour back in there. You're all right, aren't you, lad?

MARTIN:
Yes, what about you——

LUCAS:
That's right. Of course he is. He's all right.

HANS:
Vomit all over your cell, I expect. (*To* BROTHER WEINAND). But he'll have to clear that up himself, won't he?

LUCAS (*to* MARTIN):
Oh, you weren't were you? Poor old lad, well, never mind, no wonder you kept us waiting.

HANS:
Can't have his mother coming in and getting down on her knees to mop it all up.

MARTIN:
I managed to clean it up all right. How are *you,* father?

HANS (*feeling an attack, but determined not to lose the initiative*):
Me? Oh, I'm all right. I'm all right, aren't I, Lucas? Nothing ever wrong with me. Your old man's strong enough. But then that's because we've got to be, people like Lucas and me. Because if *we* aren't strong, it won't take any time at all before we're knocked flat on our backs, or flat on our knees, or flat on something or other. Flat on our backs and finished, and we can't afford to be finished because if we're finished, that's it, that's the end, so we just have to stand up to it as best we can. But that's life, isn't it?

MARTIN:
I'm never sure what people mean when they say that.

LUCAS:
Your father's doing very well indeed, Martin. He's got his own investment in the mine now, so he's beginning to work for himself if you see what I mean. That's the way things are going everywhere now.

MARTIN (*to* HANS):
You must be pleased.

HANS:
I'm pleased to make money. I'm not pleased to break my back doing it.

MARTIN:
How's mother?

HANS:
Nothing wrong there either. Too much work and too many kids for too long, that's all. (*Hiding embarrassment*). I'm sorry she couldn't come, but it's a rotten journey as you know, and all that, so she sent her love to you. Oh, yes, and there was a pie too. But I was told (*at* BROTHER WEINAND) I couldn't give it to you, but I'd have to give it to the Prior.

MARTIN:
That's the rule about gifts, father. You must have forgotten?

HANS:
Well, I hope you get a piece of it anyway. She took a lot of care over it. Oh yes, and then there was Lucas's girl, she asked to be remembered to you.

MARTIN:
Oh, good. How is she?

HANS:
Didn't she, Lucas? She asked specially to be remembered to Martin, didn't she?

LUCAS:
Oh she often talks about you, Martin. Even now. She's married you know.

MARTIN:
No, I didn't know.

LUCAS:
Oh, yes, got two children, one boy and a girl.

HANS:
That's it—two on show on the stall, and now another one coming out from under the counter again—right, Lucas?

LUCAS:
Yes, oh, she makes a fine mother.

HANS:
And what's better than that? There's only one way of going 'up you' to Old Nick when he does come for you and that's when you show him your kids. It's the one thing—that is, if you've been lucky, and the plagues kept away from you—you can spring it out from under the counter at him. *That* to you! Then you've done something for yourself forever—forever and ever. Amen. (*Pause*). Come along, Brother Martin, don't let your guests go without. Poor old Lucas is sitting there with a glass as empty as a nun's womb, aren't you, you thirsty little goosey?

MARTIN:
Oh, please, I'm sorry.

HANS:
That's right, and don't forget your old dad. (*Pause*). Yes, well, as I say, I'm sorry your mother couldn't come, but I don't suppose she'd have enjoyed it much, although I dare say she'd like to have watched her son perform the Holy Office. Isn't a mother supposed to dance with her son after the ceremony? Like Christ danced with *his* mother? Well, I can't see her doing that. I suppose you think *I'm* going to dance with you instead.

MARTIN:
You're not obliged to, father.

HANS:
It's like giving a bride away, isn't it?

MARTIN:
Not unlike.

> (*They have been avoiding any direct contact until now, but now they look at each other, and both relax a little.*)

HANS (*encouraged*):
God's eyes! Come to think of it, you look like a woman, in all that!

MARTIN (*with affection*):
Not any woman you'd want, father.

HANS:
What do *you* know about it, eh? What do you know about it? (*He laughs but not long*). Well, Brother Martin.

MARTIN:
Well? (*Pause*). Have you had some fish? Or a roast, how about that, that's what you'd like, isn't it?

HANS:
Brother Martin, old Brother Martin. Well, Brother Martin, you had a right old time up there by that altar for a bit, didn't you? I wouldn't have been in your shoes, I'll tell you. All those people listening to you, every word you're saying, watching every little tiny movement, watching for one little lousy mistake. I couldn't keep my eyes off it. We all thought you were going to flunk it for one minute there, didn't we, Lucas?

LUCAS:
Well, we had a couple of anxious moments——

HANS:
Anxious moments! I'll say there were. I thought to myself, "he's going to flunk it, he can't get through it, he's going to flunk it." What was that bit, you know, the worst bit where you stopped and Brother——

MARTIN:
Weinand.

HANS:
Weinand, yes, and he very kindly helped you up. He was actually holding you up at one point, wasn't he?

MARTIN:
Yes.

BRO. WEINAND:
It happens often enough when a young priest celebrates Mass for the first time.

HANS:
Looked as though he didn't know if it was Christmas or Wednesday. We thought the whole thing had come to a standstill for a bit, didn't we? Everyone waiting and nothing happening. What was that bit, Martin, what was it?

MARTIN:
I don't remember.

HANS:
Yes, you know, the bit you really flunked.

MARTIN (*rattling it off*):
Receive, oh Holy Father, almighty and eternal God, this spotless host, which I, thine unworthy servant, offer unto thee for my own innumerable sins of commission and omission, and for all here present and all faithful Christians, living and dead, so that it may avail for their salvation and everlasting life. When I entered the monastery, I wanted to speak to God directly, you see. Without any embarrassment, I wanted to speak to him myself, but when it came to it, I dried up—as I always have.

LUCAS:
No, you didn't, Martin, it was only for a few moments, besides——

MARTIN:
Thanks to Brother Weinand. Father, why do you hate me being here?
(HANS *is outraged at a direct question.*)

HANS:
Eh? What do you mean? I don't hate you being here.

MARTIN:
Try to give me a straight answer if you can, father. I should like you to tell me.

HANS:
What are you talking about, Brother Martin, you don't know what you're talking about. You've not had enough wine, that's your trouble.

MARTIN:
And don't say I could have been a lawyer.

HANS:
Well, so you could have been. You could have been better than that. You could have been a burgomaster, you could have been a magistrate, you could have been a chancellor, you could have been anything! So what! I don't want to talk about it. What's the matter with you! Anyway, I certainly don't want to talk about it in front of complete strangers.

MARTIN:
You make me sick.

HANS:
Oh, do I? Well, thank you for that, Brother Martin! Thank you for the truth, anyway.

MARTIN:
No, it isn't the truth. It isn't the truth at all. You're drinking too much wine—and I'm . . .

HANS:
Drinking too much wine! I could drink this convent piss from here till Gabriel's horn—and from all accounts, that'll blow about next Thursday—so what's the difference? (*Pause.* HANS *drinks.*) Is this the wine you use? Is it? Well? I'm asking a straight question myself now. Is this the wine you use? (*To* MARTIN). Here, have some.
    (MARTIN *takes it and drinks.*)
You know what they say?

MARTIN:
No, what do they say?

HANS:
I'll tell you:
        Bread thou art and wine thou art
        And always shall remain so.
    (*Pause*)

MARTIN:
My father didn't mean that. He's a very devout man, I know.
    (*Some of the* BROTHERS *have got up to leave.*)

MARTIN (*to* LUCAS):
Brother Weinand will show you over the convent. If you've finished, that is.

LUCAS:
Yes, oh yes, I'd like that. Yes, I've had more than enough, thank you. Right, well, let's go, shall we, Brother Weinand? I'll come back for you, shall I. Hans, you'll stay here?

HANS:
Just as you like.

LUCAS (*to* MARTIN):
You're looking a bit better now, lad. Good-bye, my boy, but I'll see you before I go, won't I?

MARTIN:
Yes, of course.
>   (*They all go, leaving* MARTIN *and* HANS *alone to-*
>   *gether. Pause.*)

HANS:
Martin, I didn't mean to embarrass you.

MARTIN:
No, it was my fault.

HANS:
Not in front of everyone.

MARTIN:
I shouldn't have asked you a question like that. It was a
shock to see you suddenly, after such a long time.
Most of my day's spent in silence you see, except for
the Offices; and I enjoy the singing, as you know, but
there's not much speaking, except to one's confessor.
I'd almost forgotten what your voice sounded like.

HANS:
Tell me, son—what made you get all snarled up like that
in the Mass?

MARTIN:
You're disappointed, aren't you?

HANS:
I want to know, that's all. I'm a simple man, Martin, I'm
no scholar, but I can understand all right. But you're a
learned man, you speak Latin and Greek and Hebrew.
You've been trained to remember ever since you were a
tiny boy. Men like you don't just forget their words!

MARTIN:
I don't understand what happened. I lifted up my head
at the host, and, as I was speaking the words, I heard
them as if it were the first time, and suddenly—(*pause*)
they struck at my life.

HANS:
I don't know, I really don't. Perhaps your father and mother are wrong, and God's right, after all. Perhaps. Whatever it is you've got to find, you could only find out by becoming a monk; maybe that's the answer.

MARTIN:
But you don't believe that. Do you?

HANS:
No; no I don't.

MARTIN:
Then say what you mean.

HANS:
All right, if that's what you want, I'll say just what I mean. I think a man murders himself in these places.

MARTIN (*retreating at once*):
I am holy. I kill no one but myself.

HANS:
I don't care. I tell you it gives me the creeps. And that's why I couldn't bring your mother, if you want to know.

MARTIN:
The Gospels are the only mother I've ever had.

HANS (*triumphantly*):
And haven't you ever read in the Gospels, don't you know what's written in there? "Thou shalt honour thy father and thy mother."

MARTIN:
You're not understanding me, because you don't want to.

HANS:
That's fine talk, oh yes, fine, holy talk, but it won't wash, Martin. It won't wash because you can't ever, however

you try, you can't ever get away from your body because
that's what you live in, and it's all you've got to die in,
and you can't get away from the body of your father
and your mother! We're bodies, Martin, and so are you,
and we're bound together for always. But you're like
every man who was ever born into this world, Martin.
You'd like to pretend that you made yourself, that it was
you who made you—and not the body of a woman and
another man.

MARTIN:

Churches, kings, and fathers—why do they ask so much,
and why do they all of them get so much more than they
deserve?

HANS:

You think so. Well, I think I deserve a little more than
you've given me——

MARTIN:

I've given you! I don't have to give you! I *am*—that's
all I need to give to you. That's your big reward, and
that's all you're ever going to get, and it's more than any
father's got a right to. You wanted me to learn Latin, to
be a Master of Arts, be a lawyer. All you want is me to
justify *you*! Well, I can't, and, what's more, I won't. I
can't even justify myself. So just stop asking me what
have I accomplished, and what have I done for you. I've
done all for you I'll ever do, and that's live and wait to
die.

HANS:

Why do you blame *me* for everything?

MARTIN:

I don't blame you. I'm just not grateful, that's all.

HANS:

Listen, I'm not a specially good man, I know, but I believe in God and in Jesus Christ, His Son, and the
Church will look after me, and I can make some sort of

life for myself that has a little joy in it somewhere. But where is your joy? You wrote to me once, when you were at the University, that only Christ could light up the place you live in, but what's the point? What's the point if it turns out the place you're living in is just a hovel? Don't you think it mightn't be better not to see at all?

MARTIN:
I'd rather be able to see.

HANS:
You'd rather see!

MARTIN:
You really are disappointed, aren't you? Go on.

HANS:
And why? I see a young man, learned and full of life, my son, abusing his youth with fear and humiliation. You think you're facing up to it in here, but you're not; you're running away, you're running away and you can't help it.

MARTIN:
If it's so easy in here, why do you think the rest of the world isn't knocking the gates down to get in?

HANS:
Because they haven't given up, that's why.

MARTIN:
Well, there it is: you think I've given up.

HANS:
Yes, there it is. That damned monk's piss has given me a headache.

MARTIN:
I'm sorry.

HANS:
Yes, we're all sorry, and a lot of good it does any of us.

MARTIN:
I suppose fathers and sons always disappoint each other.

HANS:
I worked for you, I went without for you.

MARTIN:
Well?

HANS:
Well! (*Almost anxiously*). And if I beat you fairly often, and pretty hard sometimes I suppose, it wasn't any more than any other boy, was it?

MARTIN:
No.

HANS:
What do you think it is makes you different? Other men are all right, aren't they? You were stubborn, you were always stubborn, you've always had to resist, haven't you?

MARTIN:
You disappointed me too, and not just a few times, but at some time of every day I ever remember hearing or seeing you, but, as you say, maybe that was also no different from any other boy. But I loved you the best. It was always *you* I wanted. I wanted your love more than anyone's, and if anyone was to hold me, I wanted it to be you. Funnily enough, my mother disappointed me the most, and I loved her less, much less. She made a gap which no one else could have filled, but all she could do was make it bigger, bigger and more unbearable.

HANS:
I don't know what any of that means; I really don't. I'd

better be going, Martin. I think it's best; and I dare say
you've got your various duties to perform.

MARTIN:
She beat me once for stealing a nut, your wife. I remember it so well, she beat me until the blood came, I was so
surprised to see it on my finger-tips; yes, stealing a nut,
that's right. But that's not the point. I had corns on my
backside already. Always before, when I was beaten for
something, the pain seemed outside of me in some way,
as if it belonged to the rest of the world, and not only me.
But, on that day, for the first time, the pain belonged to
me and no one else, it went no further than *my* body,
bent between *my* knees and *my* chin.

HANS:
You know what, Martin, I think you've always been
scared—ever since you could get up off your knees and
walk. You've been scared for the good reason that that's
what you most like to be. Yes, I'll tell you. I'll tell you
what! Like that day, that day when you were coming home
from Erfurt, and the thunderstorm broke, and you were
so piss-scared, you lay on the ground and cried out to
St. Anne because you saw a bit of lightning and thought
you'd seen a vision.

MARTIN:
I saw it all right.

HANS:
And you went and asked her to save you—on condi-
tion that you became a monk.

MARTIN:
I saw it.

HANS:
Did you? So it's still St. Anne is it? I thought you were
blaming your mother and me for your damned monkery?

MARTIN:
Perhaps I should.

HANS:
And perhaps sometime you should have another little think about that heavenly vision that wangled you away into the cloister.

MARTIN:
What's that?

HANS:
I mean: I hope it really was a vision. I hope it wasn't a delusion and some trick of the devil's. I really hope so, because I can't bear to think of it otherwise. (*Pause*) Good-bye, son. I'm sorry we had to quarrel. It shouldn't have turned out like this at all today.
    (*Pause*)

MARTIN:
Father—why did you give your consent?

HANS:
What, to your monkery, you mean?

MARTIN:
Yes. You could have refused, but why didn't you?

HANS:
Well, when your two brothers died with the plague . . .

MARTIN:
You gave me up for dead, didn't you?

HANS:
Good-bye, son. Here—have a glass of holy wine.
    (*He goes out.* MARTIN *stands, with the glass in his hand and looks into it. Then he drinks from it slowly,*

as if for the first time. He sits down at the table and sets the glass before him.)

MARTIN:
But—but what if it isn't true?

CURTAIN

(End of Act One)

DÉCOR NOTE

After the intense private interior of Act One, with its outer darkness and rich, personal objects, the physical effect from now on should be more intricate, general, less personal; sweeping, concerned with men in time rather than particular man in the unconscious; caricature not portraiture, like the popular woodcuts of the period, like DÜRER. Down by the apron in one corner there is now a heavily carved pulpit.

ACT TWO

SCENE ONE

The market place, Jüterbog, 1517. The sound of loud music, bells as a procession approaches the centre of the market place, which is covered in the banners of welcoming trade guilds. At the head of the slow-moving procession, with its lighted tapers and to the accompaniment of singing, prayers and the smoke of incense, is carried the Pontiff's bull of grace on a cushion and cloth of gold. Behind this the arms of the Pope and the Medici. After this, carrying a large red wooden cross, comes the focus of the procession, JOHN TETZEL, *Dominican, inquisitor and most famed and successful indulgence vendor of his day. He is splendidly equipped to be an ecclesiastical huckster, with alive, silver hair, the powerfully calculating voice, range and technique of a trained orator, the terrible, riveting charm of a dedicated professional able to winkle coppers out of the pockets of the poor and desperate.*

The red cross is taken from TETZEL *and established prominently behind him, and, from it are suspended the arms of the Pope.*

TETZEL:
Are you wondering who I am, or what I am? Is there anyone here among you, any small child, any cripple, or any sick idiot who hasn't heard of me, and doesn't know why I am here? No? Well, speak up then if there is? What, no one? Do you all know me then? Do you all know who I am? If it's true, it's very good, and just as it should be. Just as it should be, and no more than that! However, however—just in case—just in case, mind, there is one blind, maimed midget among you today who can't hear, I will open his ears and wash them out

with sacred soap for him! And, as for the rest of you. I
know I can rely on you all to listen patiently while I in-
struct him. Is that right? Can I go on? I'm asking you, is
that right, can I go on? I say "can I go on"?
        (*Pause*)
Thank you. And what is there to tell this blind, maimed
midget who's down there somewhere among you? No,
don't look round for him, you'll only scare him and then
he'll lose his one great chance, and it's not likely to come
again, or if it does come, maybe it'll be too late. Well,
what's the good news on this bright day? What's the in-
formation you want? It's this! Who is this friar with his
red cross? Who sent him, and what's he here for? Don't
try to work it out for yourself because I'm going to tell
you now, this very minute. I am John Tetzel, Dominican,
inquisitor, sub-commissioner to the Archbishop of Mainz,
and what I bring you is indulgences. Indulgences made
possible by the red blood of Jesus Christ, and the red
cross you see standing up here behind me is the standard
of those who carry them. Look at it! Go on, look at it!
What else do you see hanging from the red cross? Well,
what do they look like? Why, it's the arms of his holiness, because why? Because it's him who sent me here.
Yes, my friend, the Pope himself has sent me with indulgences for you! Fine, you say, but what are indulgences? And what are they to me? What are indulgences?
They're only the most precious and noble of Gods gifts to
men, that's all they are! Before God, I tell you I wouldn't
swap my privilege at this moment with that of St. Peter
in Heaven because I've already saved more souls with
my indulgences than he could ever have done with all his
sermons. You think that's bragging, do you? Well, listen
a little more carefully, my friend, because this concerns
you! Just look at it this way. For every mortal sin you
commit, the Church says that after confession and con-
trition, you've got to do penance—either in this life or in
purgatory—for seven years. Seven years! Right? Are you
with me? Good. Now then, how many mortal sins are
committed by you—by you—in a single day? Just think
for one moment: in one single day of your life. Do you
know the answer? Oh, not so much as one a day. Very

well then, how many in a month? How many in six
months? How many in a year? And how many in a whole
lifetime? Yes, you needn't shuffle your feet—it doesn't
bear thinking about, does it? You couldn't even add up
all those years without a merchant's clerk to do it for
you! Try and add up all the years of torment piling up!
What about it? And isn't there anything you can do
about this terrible situation you're in? Do you really
want to know? Yes! There is something, and that something I have here with me now up here, letters, letters of
indulgence. Hold up the letters so that everyone can see
them. Is there anyone so small he can't see? Look at
them, all properly sealed, an indulgence in every en-
velope, and one of them can be yours today, now, before
it's too late! Come on, come up as close as you like, you
won't squash me so easily. Take a good look. There isn't
any one sin so big that one of these letters can't remit it.
I challenge any one here, any member of this audience,
to present me with a sin, anything, any kind of a sin, I
don't care what it is, that I can't settle for him with
one of these precious little envelopes. Why, if any one
had ever offered violence to the blessed Virgin Mary,
Mother of God, if he'd only pay up—as long as he paid
up all he could—he'd find himself forgiven. You think
I'm exaggerating? You do, do you? Well, I'm authorized
to go even further than that. Not only am I empowered
to give you these letters of pardon for the sins you've already committed, I can give you pardon for those sins
you haven't even committed (*pause . . . then slowly*)
but, which, however you *intend* to commit! But, you
ask—and it's a fair question—but, you ask, why is our
Holy Lord prepared to distribute such a rich grace to
me? The answer, my friends, is all too simple. It's so
that we can restore the ruined church of St. Peter and
St. Paul in Rome! So that it won't have its equal anywhere in the world. This great church contains the bodies
not only of the holy apostles Peter and Paul, but of a
hundred thousand martyrs and no less than forty-six
popes! To say nothing of the relics like St. Veronica's
handkerchief, the burning bush of Moses and the very
rope with which Judas Iscariot hanged himself! But, alas,

this fine old building is threatened with destruction, and all these things with it, if a sufficient restoration fund isn't raised, and raised soon. (*With passionate irony*) . . . Will anyone dare to say that the cause is not a good one? (*Pause.*) . . . Very well, and won't you, for as little as one quarter of a florin, my friend, buy yourself one of these letters, so that in the hour of death, the gate through which sinners enter the world of torment shall be closed against you, and the gate leading to the joy of paradise be flung open for you? And, remember this, these letters aren't just for the living but for the dead too. There can't be one amongst you who hasn't at least one dear one who has departed—and to who knows what? Why, these letters are for them too. It isn't even necessary to repent. So don't hold back, come forward, think of your dear ones, think of yourselves! For twelve groats, or whatever it is we think you can afford, you can rescue your father from agony and yourself from certain disaster. And if you only have the coat on your back to call your own, then strip it off, strip it off now so that you too can obtain grace. For remember: As soon as your money rattles in the box and the cash bell rings, the soul flies out of purgatory and sings! So, come on then. Get your money out! What is it then, have your wits flown away with your faith? Listen then, soon, I shall take down the cross, shut the gates of heaven, and put out the brightness of this sun of grace that shines on you here today.

(*He flings a large coin into the open strong box, where it rattles furiously.*)

The Lord our God reigns no longer. He has resigned all power to the Pope. In the name of the Father, and of the Son and of the Holy Ghost. Amen.

(*The sound of coins clattering like rain into a great coffer as the light fades.*)

(*End of Act Two—Scene One*)

ACT TWO

Scene Two

The Eremite Cloister, Wittenberg. 1517. Seated beneath a single pear tree is JOHANN VON STAUPITZ, *Vicar General of the Augustinian Order. He is a quiet, gentle-voiced man in late middle age, almost stolidly contemplative. He has profound respect for Martin, recognizing in him the powerful potential of insight, sensitivity, courage and, also heroics that is quite outside the range of his own endeavour. However, he also understands that a man of his own limitations can offer a great deal to such a young man at this point in his development, and his treatment of Martin is a successful astringent mixture of sympathy and ridicule. Birds sing as he reads in the shade, and* MARTIN *approaches, prostrating himself.* STAUPITZ *motions him to his feet.*

MARTIN (*looking up*):
The birds always seem to fly away the moment I come out here.

STAUPITZ:
Birds, unfortunately, have no faith.

MARTIN:
Perhaps it's simply that they don't like me.

STAUPITZ:
They haven't learned yet that you mean them no harm, that's all.

MARTIN:
Are you treating me to one of your allegories?

61

STAUPITZ:
Well, you recognized it, anyway.

MARTIN:
I ought to. Ever since I came into the cloister, I've become a craftsman allegory maker myself. Only last week I was lecturing on Galatians Three, verse three, and I allegorized going to the lavatory.

STAUPITZ (*quoting the verse*):
"Are ye so foolish, that ye have begun in the spirit, you would now end in the flesh."

MARTIN:
That's right. But allegories aren't much help in theology —except to decorate a house that's been already built by argument.

STAUPITZ:
Well, it's a house you've been able to unlock for a great many of us. I never dreamed when I first came here that the University's reputation would ever become what it has, and in such a short time, and it's mostly due to you.

MARTIN (*very deliberately turning the compliment*):
If ever a man could get to heaven through monkery, that man would be me.

STAUPITZ:
I don't mean that. You know quite well what I mean. I'm talking about your scholarship, and what you manage to do with it, not your monkishness as you call it. I've never had any patience with all your mortifications. The only wonder is that you haven't killed yourself with your prayers, and watchings, yes and even your reading too. All these trials and temptations you go through, they're meat and drink to you.

MARTIN (*patient*):
Will you ever stop lecturing me about this?

STAUPITZ:
Of course not, why do you think you come here—to see me in the garden when you could be inside working?

MARTIN:
Well, if it'll please you, I've so little time, what with my lectures and study, I'm scarcely able to carry out even the basic requirements of the Rule.

STAUPITZ:
I'm delighted to hear it. Why do you think you've always been obsessed with the Rule? No, I don't want to hear all your troubles again. I'll tell you why: you're obsessed with the Rule because it serves very nicely as a protection for you.

MARTIN:
What protection?

STAUPITZ:
You know perfectly well what I mean, Brother Martin, so don't pretend to look innocent. Protection against the demands of your own instincts, that's what. You see, you think you admire authority, and so you do, but unfortunately, you can't submit to it. So, what you do, by your exaggerated attention to the Rule, you make the authority ridiculous. And the reason you do that is because you're determined to substitute that authority with something else—yourself. Oh, come along, Martin, I've been Vicar General too long not to have made that little discovery. Anyway, you shouldn't be too concerned with a failing like that. It also provides the strongest kind of security.

MARTIN:
Security? I don't feel *that*.

STAUPITZ:
I dare say, but you've got it all the same, which is more than most of us have.

MARTIN:
And how have I managed to come by this strange security?

STAUPITZ:
Quite simply: by demanding an impossible standard of perfection.

MARTIN:
I don't see what work or merit can come from a heart like mine.

STAUPITZ:
Oh, my dear, dear friend, I've sworn a thousand times to our holy God to live piously, and have I been able to keep my vows? No, of course I haven't. Now I've given up making solemn promises because I know I'm not able to keep them. If God won't be merciful to me for the love of Christ when I leave this world, then I shan't stand before Him on account of all my vows and good works, I shall perish, that's all.

MARTIN:
You think I lavish too much attention on my own pain, don't you?

STAUPITZ:
Well, that's difficult for me to say, Martin. We're very different kinds of men, you and I. Yes, you do lavish attention on yourself, but then a large man is worth the pains he takes. Like St. Paul, some men must say "I die daily".

MARTIN:
Tell me, Father, have you never felt humiliated to find that you belong to a world that's dying?

STAUPITZ:
No, I don't think I have.

MARTIN:
Surely, this must be the last age of time we're living in.
There can't be any more left but the black bottom of
the bucket.

STAUPITZ:
Do you mean the Last Judgment?

MARTIN:
No. I don't mean that. The Last Judgment isn't to come.
It's here and now.

STAUPITZ:
Good. That's a little better, anyway.

MARTIN:
I'm like a ripe stool in the world's straining anus, and at
any moment we're about to let each other go.

STAUPITZ:
There's nothing new in the world being damned, dying or
without hope. It's always been like that, and it'll stay like
it. What's the matter with you? What are you making
funny faces for?

MARTIN:
It's nothing, Father, just a—a slight discomfort.

STAUPITZ:
Slight discomfort? What are you holding your stomach
for? Are you in pain?

MARTIN:
It's all right. It's gone now.

STAUPITZ:
I don't understand you. What's gone now? I've seen
you grabbing at yourself like that before. What is it?

MARTIN:
I'm—constipated.

STAUPITZ:
Constipated? There's always something the matter with you, Brother Martin. If it's not the gripes, insomnia, or faith and works, it's boils or indigestion or some kind of belly-ache you've got. All these severe fasts——

MARTIN:
That's what my father says.

STAUPITZ:
Your father sounds pretty sensible to me.

MARTIN:
He is, and you know, he's a theologian too, I've discovered lately.

STAUPITZ:
I thought he was a miner.

MARTIN:
So he is, but he made a discovery years and years ago that took me sweat and labour to dig out of the earth for myself.

STAUPITZ:
Well, that's no surprise. There's always some chunk of truth buried down away somewhere which lesser men will always reach with less effort.

MARTIN:
Anyway, he always knew that works alone don't save any man. Mind you, he never said anything about faith coming first.

STAUPITZ (*quoting*):
"Oh, well, that's life, and nothing you can do's going to change it."

MARTIN:
The same speech.

STAUPITZ:
You can't change human nature.

MARTIN:
Nor can you.

STAUPITZ:
That's right, Martin, and you've demonstrated it only too well in your commentaries on the Gospels and St. Paul. But don't overlook the fact that your father's taken a vow of poverty too, even though it's very different from your own. And he took it the day he told himself, and told *you*, that he was a complete man, or at least, a contented man.

MARTIN:
A hog waffling in its own crap is contented.

STAUPITZ:
Exactly.

MARTIN:
My father, faced with an unfamiliar notion is like a cow staring at a new barn door. Like those who look on the cross and see nothing. All they hear is the priest's forgiveness.

STAUPITZ:
One thing I promise you, Martin. You'll never be a spectator. You'll always take part.

MARTIN:
How is it you always manage somehow to comfort me?

STAUPITZ:
I think some of us are not much more than pretty modest sponges, but we're probably best at quenching big thirsts. How's your tummy?

MARTIN:
Better.

STAUPITZ:
One mustn't be truly penitent because one anticipates
God's forgiveness, but because one already possesses it.
You have to sink to the bottom of your black bucket because that's where God judges you, and then look to the
wounds of Jesus Christ. You told me once that when you
entered the cloister, your father said it was like giving
away a bride, and again your father was right. You are a
bride and you should hold yourself ready like a woman
at conception. And when grace comes and your soul is
penetrated by the spirit, you shouldn't pray or exert yourself, but remain passive.

MARTIN (*smiles*):
That's a hard role.

STAUPITZ (*smiles too*):
Too hard for you, I dare say. Did you know the Duke's
been complaining to me about you?

MARTIN:
Why, what have I done?

STAUPITZ:
Preaching against indulgences again.

MARTIN:
Oh, that—I was very mild.

STAUPITZ:
Yes, well I've heard your mildness in the pulpit. When I
think sometimes of the terror it used to be for you, you
used to fall up the steps with fright. Sheer fright! You
were too frightened to become a Doctor of Theology,
and you wouldn't be now if I hadn't forced you. "I'm
too weak, I'm not strong enough. I shan't live long
enough!" Do you remember what I said to you?

MARTIN:
"Never mind, the Lord still has work in heaven, and there
are always vacancies."

STAUPITZ:

Yes, and the Duke paid all the expenses of your promotion for you. He was very cross when he spoke to me, I may say. He said you even made some reference to the collection of holy relics in the Castle Church, and most of those were paid for by the sale of indulgences, as you know. Did you say anything about them?

MARTIN:

Well, yes, but not about those in the Castle Church. I did make some point in passing about someone who claimed to have a feather from the wing of the angel Gabriel.

STAUPITZ:

Oh yes, I heard about him.

MARTIN:

And the Archbishop of Mainz, who is supposed to have a flame from Moses' burning bush.

STAUPITZ:

Oh dear, you shouldn't have mentioned that.

MARTIN:

And I just finished off by saying how does it happen that Christ had twelve apostles and eighteen of them are buried in Germany?

STAUPITZ:

Well, the Duke says he's coming to your next sermon to hear for himself, so try to keep off the subject, if you possibly can. It's All Saints' Day soon, remember, and all those relics will be out on show for everyone to gawp at. The Duke's a good chap, and he's very proud of his collection, and it doesn't help to be rude about it.

MARTIN:

I've tried to keep off the subject because I haven't been by any means sure about it. Then I did make a few mild protests in a couple of sermons, as I say.

STAUPITZ:
Yes, yes, but what did you actually say?

MARTIN:
That you can't strike bargains with God. There's a Jewish, Turkish, Pelagian heresy if you like.

STAUPITZ:
Yes, more mildness. Go on.

MARTIN:
I said, oh it was an evil sanction because only *you* could live *your* life, and only you can die your death. It can't be taken over for you. Am I right?

STAUPITZ (*doubtfully*):
Yes, what's difficult to understand is why your sermons are so popular.

MARTIN:
Well, there are plenty who sit out there stiff with hatred, I can tell you. I can see their faces, and there's no mistaking them. But I wanted to tell you something——

STAUPITZ:
Yes?

MARTIN:
About all this. The other day a man was brought to me, a shoemaker. His wife had just died, and I said to him, "What've you done for her?" so he said, "I've buried her and commended her soul to God." "But haven't you had a Mass said for the repose of her soul?" "No," he said, "what's the point? She entered heaven the moment she died." So I asked him, "How do you know that?" And he said, "Well, I've got proof, that's why." And out of his pocket he took a letter of indulgence.

STAUPITZ:
Ah.

MARTIN:
He threw it at me, and said, "And if you still maintain
that a Mass is necessary, then my wife's been swindled
by our most holy father the Pope. Or, if not by him, then
by the priest who sold it to me."

STAUPITZ:
Tetzel.

MARTIN:
Who else?

STAUPITZ:
That old tout!

MARTIN:
There's another story going around about him which is
obviously true because I've checked it at several sources.
It seems that a certain Saxon nobleman had heard Tetzel
in Jüterbog. After Tetzel had finished his usual performance, he asked him if he'd repeat what he'd said at one
stage, that he—Tetzel I mean—had the power of par-
doning sins that men intended to commit. Tetzel was
very high and mighty, you know what he's like, and said,
"What's the matter, weren't you listening? Of course I
can give pardon not only for sins already committed but
for sins that men *intend* to commit." "Well, then, that's
fine," says this nobleman, "because I'd like to take revenge on one of my enemies. You know, nothing much,
I don't want to kill him or anything like that. Just a little
slight revenge. Now, if I give you ten guilden, will you
give me a letter of indulgence that will justify me—
justify me freely and completely?" Well, it seems Tetzel
made a few stock objections, but eventually agreed on
thirty guilden, and they made a deal. The man went away
with his letter of indulgence, and Tetzel set out for the
next job, which was Leipzig. Well, half-way between
Leipzig and Treblen, in the middle of a wood, he was
set on by a band of thugs, and beaten up. While he's
lying there on the grass in a pool of his own blood, he
looks up and sees that one of them is the Saxon noble-

man and that they're making off with his great trunk full
of money. So, the moment he's recovered enough, he
rushes back to Jüterbog, and takes the nobleman to
court. And what does the nobleman do? Takes out the
letter of indulgence and shows it to Duke George himself—case dismissed!

STAUPITZ (*laughing*):
Well, I leave you to handle it. But try and be careful.
Remember, *I* agree with all you say, but the moment
someone disagrees or objects to what you're saying, *that*
will be the moment when you'll suddenly recognize the
strength of your belief!

MARTIN:
Father, I'm never sure of the words till I hear them out
loud.

STAUPITZ:
Well, that's probably the meaning of the Word. The Word
is me, and I am the Word. Anyway, try and be a little
prudent. Look at Erasmus: he never really gets into any
serious trouble, but he still manages to make his point.

MARTIN:
People like Erasmus get upset because I talk of pigs
and Christ in the same breath. I must go. (*Clutches
himself unobtrusively.*)

STAUPITZ:
Well, you might be right. Erasmus is a fine scholar, but
there are too many scholars who think they're better
simply because they insinuate in Latin what you'll say in
plain German. What's the matter, are you having that
trouble again? Good heavens! Martin—just before you
go: a man with a strong sword will draw it at some time,
even if it's only to turn it on himself. But whatever happens, he can't just let it dangle from his belt. And, another thing, don't forget—you began this affair in the
name of Our Lord Jesus Christ. You must do as God
commands you, of course, but remember, St. Jerome

once wrote about a philosopher who destroyed his own
eyes so that it would give him more freedom to study.
Take care of your eyes, my son, and do something about
those damned bowels!

MARTIN:
I will. Who knows? If I break wind in Wittenberg, they
might smell it in Rome.
    (*Exit. Church bells.*)

        (*End of Act Two—Scene Two*)

ACT TWO

SCENE THREE

The steps of the Castle Church, Wittenberg, October 31st, 1517. From inside the Church comes the sound of Matins being sung. Sitting on the steps is a child, dirty, half-naked and playing intently by himself. MARTIN *enters with a long roll of paper. It is his ninety-five theses for disputation against indulgences. As he goes up the steps, he stops and watches the child, absorbed in his private fantasy. He is absorbed by the child, who doesn't notice him at first, but, presently, as soon as the boy becomes aware of an intruder, he immediately stops playing and looks away distractedly in an attempt to exclude outside attention.* MARTIN *hesitates briefly, then puts out his hand to the child, who looks at it gravely and deliberately, then slowly, not rudely, but naturally, gets up and skips away sadly out of sight.* MARTIN *watches him, then walks swiftly back down the steps to the pulpit and ascends it.*

MARTIN:
My text is from the Epistle of Paul the Apostle to the Romans, chapter one, verse seventeen: "For therein is the righteousness of God revealed from faith to faith."
    (*Pause*)
We are living in a dangerous time. You may not think so, but it could be that this is the most dangerous time since the light first broke upon the earth. It may not be true, but it's very probably true—but, what's most important is that it's an assumption we are obliged to make. We Christians seem to be wise outwardly and mad inwardly, and in this Jerusalem we have built there are blasphemies flourishing that make the Jews no worse than giggling children. A man is not a good Christian

74

because he understands Greek and Hebrew. Jerome knew
five languages, but he's inferior to Augustine, who knew
only one. Of course, Erasmus wouldn't agree with me, but
perhaps one day the Lord will open his eyes for him. But
listen! A man without Christ becomes his own shell. We
are content with shells. Some shells are whole men and
some are small trinkets. And, what are the trinkets? Today is the eve of All Saints, and the holy relics will be
on show to you all; to the hungry ones whose lives are
made satisfied by trinkets, by an imposing procession and
the dressings up of all kinds of dismal things. You'll
mumble for magic with lighted candles to St. Anthony
for your erysipelas; to St. Valentine for your epilepsy; to
St. Sebastian for the pestilence; to St. Laurentis to protect
you from fire, to St. Apollonia if you've got the tooth-
ache, and to St. Louis to stop your beer from going
sour. And tomorrow you'll queue for hours outside the
Castle Church so that you can get a cheap-rate glimpse of
St. Jerome's tooth, or four pieces each of St. Chrysostom
and St. Augustine, and six of St. Bernard. The deacons
will have to link hands to hold you back while you struggle to gawp at four hairs from Our Lady's head, at the
pieces of her girdle and her veil stained with her Son's
blood. You'll sleep outside with the garbage in the streets
all night so that you can stuff your eyes like roasting
birds on a scrap of swaddling clothes, eleven pieces from
the original crib, one wisp of straw from the manger
and a gold piece specially minted by three wise men for
the occasion. Your emptiness will be frothing over at
the sight of a strand of Jesus' beard, at one of the nails
driven into His hands, and at the remains of the loaf at the
Last Supper. Shells for shells, empty things for empty
men. There are some who complain of these things, but
they write in Latin for scholars. Who'll speak out in rough
German? Someone's got to bell the cat! For you must be
made to know that there's no security, there's no security
at all, either in indulgences, holy busywork or anywhere
in this world. It came to me while I was in my tower,
what they call the monk's sweathouse, the jakes, the john
or whatever you're pleased to call it. I was struggling
with the text I've given you: "For therein is the righteous-

ness of God revealed, from faith to faith; as it is written,
the just shall live by faith." And seated there, my head
down, on that privy just as when I was a little boy, I
couldn't reach down to my breath for the sickness in my
bowels, as I seemed to sense beneath me a large rat, a
heavy, wet, plague rat, slashing at my privates with its
death's teeth. (*He kneads his knuckles into his abdomen,
as if he were suppressing pain. His face runs with sweat.*)
I thought of the righteousness of God, and wished his
gospel had never been put to paper for men to read;
who demanded my love and made it impossible to return it. And I sat in my heap of pain until the words
emerged and opened out. "The just shall live by faith."
My pain vanished, my bowels flushed and I could get up.
I could see the life I'd lost. No man is just because he
does just works. The works are just if the man is just. If a
man doesn't believe in Christ, not only are his sins mortal,
but his good works. This I know; reason is the devil's
whore, born of one stinking goat called Aristotle, which
believes that good works make a good man. But the
truth is that the just shall live by faith alone. I need
no more than my sweet redeemer and meditator, Jesus
Christ, and I shall praise Him as long as I have voice to
sing; and if anyone doesn't care to sing with me, then he
can howl on his own. If we are going to be deserted, let's
follow the deserted Christ.

(*He murmurs a prayer, descends from the pulpit,
then walks up the steps to the Church door, and
nails his theses to it. The singing from within grows
louder as he walks away.*)

(*End of Act Two—Scene Three*)

ACT TWO

Scene Four

The Fugger Palace, Augsburg. October 1518. As a backcloth a satirical contemporary woodcut, showing, for example, the Pope portrayed as an ass playing the bagpipes, or a cardinal dressed up as a court fool. Or perhaps Holbein's cartoon of Luther with the Pope suspended from his nose. However, there is a large area for the director and designer to choose from.

Seated at a table is THOMAS DE VIO, *known as Cajetan, Cardinal of San Sisto, General of the Dominican Order, as well as its most distinguished theologian, papal legate, Rome's highest representative in Germany. He is about fifty, but youthful, with a shrewd, broad, outlook, quite the opposite of the vulgar bigotry of* TETZEL, *who enters.*

TETZEL:
He's here.

CAJETAN:
So I see.

TETZEL:
What do you mean?

CAJETAN:
You look so cross. Is Staupitz with him?

TETZEL:
Yes. At least *he's* polite.

CAJETAN:
I know Staupitz. He's a straightforward, four-square kind of a man, and probably very unhappy at this moment.

77

From all accounts, he has a deep regard for this monk
—which is all to the good from our point of view.

TETZEL:
He's worried all right, you can see that. These Augustinians, they don't have much fibre.

CAJETAN:
What about Dr. Luther? What's he got to say for himself?

TETZEL:
Too much. I said to him if our Lord the Pope were to
offer you a good Bishopric and a plenary indulgence for
repairing your church, you'd soon start singing a different
song.

CAJETAN:
Dear, oh, dear, and what did he say to that?

TETZEL:
He asked me——

CAJETAN:
Well?

TETZEL:
He asked me how was my mother's syphilis.

CAJETAN:
It's a fair question in the circumstances. You Germans,
you're a crude lot.

TETZEL:
He's a pig.

CAJETAN:
I've no doubt. After all, it's what your country's most
famous for.

TETZEL:
That's what I said to him—you're not on your own ground here, you know. These Italians, they're different. They're not just learned, they're subtle, experienced antagonists. You'll get slung in the fire after five minutes.

CAJETAN:
And?

TETZEL:
He said, "I've only been to Italy once, and they didn't look very subtle to me. They were lifting their legs on street corners like dogs."

CAJETAN:
I hope he didn't see any cardinals at it. Knowing some of them as I do, it's not impossible. Well, let's have a look at this foul-mouthed monk of yours.

TETZEL:
What about Staupitz?

CAJETAN:
Let him wait in the corridor. It'll help him to worry.

TETZEL:
Very well, your eminence. I hope he behaves properly. I've spoken to him.
(TETZEL *goes out and returns presently with* MARTIN, *who advances, prostrates himself, his face to the ground before* CAJETAN. CAJETAN *makes a motion and* MARTIN *rises to a kneeling position, where* CAJETAN *studies him.*)

CAJETAN (*courteous*):
Please stand up, Dr. Luther. So you're the one they call the excessive doctor. You don't look excessive to me. Do you feel very excessive?

MARTIN (*conscious of being patronized*):
It's one of those words which can be used like a harness on a man.

CAJETAN:
How do you mean?

MARTIN:
I mean it has very little meaning beyond traducing him.

CAJETAN:
Quite. There's never been any doubt in my mind that you've been misinterpreted all round, and, as you say, traduced. Well, what a surprise you are! Here was I expecting to see some doddering old theologian with dust in his ears who could be bullied into a heart attack by Tetzel here in half an hour. And here you are, as gay and sprightly as a young bull. How old are you, my son?

MARTIN:
Thirty-four, most worthy father.

CAJETAN:
Tetzel, he's a boy—you didn't tell me! And how long have you been wearing your doctor's ring?

MARTIN:
Five years——

CAJETAN:
So you were only twenty-nine! Well, obviously, everything I've heard about you is true—you must be a very remarkable young man. I wouldn't have believed there was one doctor in the whole of Germany under fifty. Would you, Brother John?

TETZEL:
Not as far as I know.

CAJETAN:
I'm certain there isn't. What is surprising, frankly, is

that they allowed such an honour to be conferred on anyone so young and inexperienced as a man must inevitably be at twenty-nine.

(*He smiles to let his point get home.*)

Your father must be a proud man.

MARTIN (*irritated*):
Not at all, I should say he was disappointed and constantly apprehensive.

CAJETAN:
Really? Well, that's surely one of the legacies of parenthood to offset the incidental pleasures. Now then, to business. I was saying to Tetzel, I don't think this matter need take up very much of our time. But, before we do start, there's just one thing I would like to say, and that is I was sorry you should have decided to ask the Emperor for safe conduct. That was hardly necessary, my son, and it's a little—well, distressing to feel you have such an opinion of us, such a lack of trust in your Mother Church, and in those who have, I can assure you, your dearest interests at heart.

MARTIN (*out-manœuvred*):
I——

CAJETAN (*kindly*):
But never mind all that now, that's behind us, and, in the long run, it's unimportant, after all, isn't it? Your Vicar General has come with you, hasn't he?

MARTIN:
He's outside.

CAJETAN:
I've known Staupitz for years. You have a wonderful friend there.

MARTIN:
I know. I—have great love for him.

CAJETAN:
And he certainly has for you, I know. Oh my dear, dear
son, this is such a ridiculous, unnecessary business for us
all to be mixed up in. It's such a tedious, upsetting affair,
and what purpose is there in it? Your entire order in
Germany has been brought into disgrace. Staupitz is an
old man, and he can't honestly be expected to cope. Not
now. I have my job to do, and, make no mistake, it isn't
all honey for an Italian legate in your country. You know
how it is, people are inclined to resent you. Nationalist
feeling and all that—which I respect—but it does com-
plicate one's task to the point where this kind of issue
thrown in for good measure simply makes the whole op-
eration impossible. You know what I mean? I mean,
there's your Duke Frederick, an absolutely fair, honest
man, if ever there was one, and one his holiness values
and esteems particularly. Well, he instructed me to present him with the Golden Rose of Virtue, so you can
see . . . As well as even more indulgences for his Castle
Church. But what happens now? Because of all this un-
pleasantness and the uproar it's caused throughout Germany, the Duke's put in an extremely difficult position
about accepting it. Naturally, he wants to do the right
thing by everyone. But he's not going to betray you or
anything like that, however much he's set his heart on
that Golden Rose, even after all these years. And, of
course he's perfectly right. I know he has the greatest regard for you and for some of your ideas—even though,
as he's told me—he doesn't agree with a lot of them.
No, I can only respect him for all that. So, you see, my
dear son, what a mess we are in. Now, what are we going
to do? Um? The Duke is unhappy. I am unhappy, his
holiness is unhappy, and, you, my son, you are unhappy.

MARTIN (*formal, as if it were a prepared speech*):
Most worthy father, in obedience to the summons of his
papal holiness, and in obedience to the orders of my
gracious lord, the Elector of Saxony, I have come before
you as a submissive and dutiful son of the holy Christian
church, and acknowledge that I have published the propo-
sition and theses ascribed to me. I am ready now to listen

most obediently to my indictment, and if I have been
wrong, to submit to your instruction in the truth.

CAJETAN (*impatient*):
My son, you have upset all Germany with your dispute
about indulgences. I know you're a very learned doctor
of the Holy Scriptures, and that you've already aroused
some supporters. However, if you wish to remain a member of the Church, and to find a gracious father in the
Pope, you'd better listen. I have here, in front of me,
three propositions which, by the command of our holy
father, Pope Leo the Tenth, I shall put to you now. First,
you must admit your faults, and retract all your errors
and sermons. Secondly, you must promise to abstain from
propagating your opinions at any time in the future. And,
thirdly, you must behave generally with greater modera-
tion, and avoid anything which might cause offence or
grieve and disturb the Church.

MARTIN:
May I be allowed to see the Pope's instruction?

CAJETAN:
No, my dear son, you may not. All you are required to
do is confess your errors, keep a strict watch on your
words, and not go back like a dog to his vomit. Then,
once you have done that, I have been authorized by our
most holy father to put everything to rights again.

MARTIN:
I understand all that. But I'm asking you to tell me
where I have erred.

CAJETAN: If you insist. (*Rattling off, very fast.*) Just to
begin with, here are two propositions you have advanced,
and which you will have to retract before anything else.
First, the treasure of indulgences does not consist of the
sufferings and torments of our Lord Jesus Christ. Second,
the man who received the holy sacrament must have
faith in the grace that is presented to him. Enough?

MARTIN:
I rest my case entirely on Holy Scriptures.

CAJETAN:
The Pope alone has power and authority over all those
things.

MARTIN:
Except Scripture.

CAJETAN:
Including Scripture. What do you mean?

TETZEL:
Only the Pope has the right of deciding in matters of
Christian faith. He alone and no one else has the power
to interpret the meaning of Scripture, and to approve or
condemn the views of other men, whoever they are—
scholars, councils or the ancient fathers. The Pope's
judgement cannot err, whether it concerns the Christian
faith or anything that has to do with the salvation of
the human race.

MARTIN:
That sounds like your theses.

TETZEL:
Burned in the market place by your students in Wittenberg—thank you very much——

MARTIN:
I assure you, I had nothing to do with that.

CAJETAN:
Of course. Brother John wasn't suggesting you had.

MARTIN:
I can't stop the mouth of the whole world.

TETZEL:
Why, your heresy isn't even original. It's no different from Wyclif or Hus.

CAJETAN:
True enough, but we mustn't try to deprive the learned doctor of his originality. An original heresy may have been thought of by someone else before you. In fact, I shouldn't think such a thing as an original heresy exists. But it is original so long as it originated in *you,* the virgin heretic.

TETZEL:
The time'll come when you'll have to defend yourself before the world, and then every man can judge for himself who's the heretic and schismatic. It'll be clear to everyone, even those drowsy snoring Christians who've never smelled a Bible. They'll find out for themselves that those who scribble books and waste so much paper just for their own pleasure, and are contemptuous and shameless, end up by condemning themselves. People like you always go too far, thank heaven. You play into our hands. I give you a month, Brother Martin, to roast yourself.

MARTIN:
You've had your thirty pieces of silver. For the sake of Christ, why don't you betray someone?

CAJETAN (*to* TETZEL):
Perhaps you should join Staupitz.

TETZEL:
Very well, your eminence.
        (*He bows and goes out.*)

CAJETAN:
In point of fact, he gets eighty guilden a month plus expenses.

MARTIN:
What about his vow of poverty?

CAJETAN:
Like most brilliant men, my son, you have an innocent
spirit. I've also just discovered that he has managed to
father two children. So there goes another vow. Bang!
But it'll do him no good, I promise you. You've made a
hole in that drum for him. I may say there's a lot of bad
feelings among the Dominicans about you. I should know
—because I'm their General. It's only natural, they're ac-
customed to having everything their own way. The Franciscans are a grubby, sentimental lot, on the whole, and
mercifully ignorant as well. But your people seem to be
running alive with scholars and would-be politicians.

MARTIN:
I'd no idea that my theses would ever get such pub-
licity.

CAJETAN:
Really now!

MARTIN:
But it seems they've been printed over and over again,
and circulated well, to an extent I'd never dreamed of.

CAJETAN:
Oh yes, they've been circulated and talked about wherever men kneel to Christ.

MARTIN:
Most holy father, I honour the Holy Roman Church, and
I shall go on doing so. I have sought after the truth, and
everything I have said I still believe to be right and true
and Christian. But I am a man, and I may be deceived,
so I am willing to receive instruction where I have been
mistaken——

CAJETAN (*angrily*):
Save your arrogance, my son, there'll be a better place
to use it. I can have you sent to Rome and let any of your
German princes try to stop me! He'll find himself standing outside the gates of heaven like a leper.

MARTIN (*stung*):
I repeat, I am here to reply to all the charges you may
bring against me——

CAJETAN:
No, you're not——

MARTIN:
I am ready to submit my theses to the universities of
Basle, Freibourg, Louvain or Paris——

CAJETAN:
I'm afraid you've not grasped the position. I'm not here
to enter into a disputation with you, now or at any other
time. The Roman Church is the apex of the world,
secular and temporal, and it may constrain with its
secular arm any who have once received the faith and
gone astray. Surely I don't have to remind you that it is
not bound to use reason to fight and destroy rebels. (*He
sighs.*) My son, it's getting late. You must retract. Believe me, I simply want to see this business ended as
quickly as possible.

MARTIN:
Some interests are furthered by finding truth, others by
destroying it. I don't care—what pleases or displeases the
Pope. He is a man.

CAJETAN (*wearily*):
Is that all?

MARTIN:
He seems a good man, as Popes go. But it's not much
for a world that sings out for reformation. I'd say that's
a hymn for everyone.

CAJETAN:
My dear friend, think, think carefully, and see if you
can't see some way out of all this. I am more than prepared to reconcile you with the Church, and the sovereign

bishop. Retract, my son, the holy father prays for
it——

MARTIN:
But won't you discuss——

CAJETAN:
Discuss! I've not *discussed* with you, and I don't intend
to. If you want a disputation, I dare say Eck will take
care of you——

MARTIN:
John Eck? The Chancellor of Ingolstadt?

CAJETAN:
I suppose you don't think much of him?

MARTIN:
He knows theology.

CAJETAN:
He has a universal reputation in debate.

MARTIN:
It's understandable. He has a pedestrian style and a ju-
dicial restraint and that'll always pass off as wisdom to
most men.

CAJETAN:
You mean he's not original, like you——

MARTIN:
I'm not an original man, why I'm not even a teacher, and
I'm scarcely even a priest. I know Jesus Christ doesn't
need my labour or my services.

CAJETAN:
All right, Martin, I *will* argue with you if you want me to,
or, at least, I'll put something to you, because there is
something more than your safety or your life involved,
something bigger than you and I talking together in this

room at this time. Oh, it's fine for someone like you to criticize and start tearing down Christendom, but tell me this, just tell me this: what will you build in its place?

MARTIN:
A withered arm is best amputated, an infected place is best scoured out, and so you pray for healthy tissue and something sturdy and clean that was crumbling and full of filth.

CAJETAN:
Can't you see? My son, you'll destroy the perfect unity of the world.

MARTIN:
Someone always prefers what's withered and infected. But it should be cauterized as honestly as one knows how.

CAJETAN:
And how honest is that? There's something I'd like to know: suppose you *did* destroy the Pope. What do you think would become of you?

MARTIN:
I don't know.

CAJETAN:
Exactly, you wouldn't know what to do because you need him, Martin, you need to hunt him more than he needs his silly wild boar. Well? There have always been Popes, and there always will be, even if they're called something else. They'll have them for people like *you*. You're not a good old revolutionary, my son, you're just a common rebel, a very different animal. You don't fight the Pope because he's too big, but because for your needs he's not big enough.

MARTIN:
My General's been gossiping——

CAJETAN (*contemptuous*):
I don't need Staupitz to explain you to me. Why, some
deluded creature might even come to you as a leader of
their revolution, but you don't want to break rules, you
want to make them. You'd be a master breaker and
maker and no one would be able to stand up to you,
you'd hope, or ever sufficiently repair the damage you
did. I've read some of your sermons on faith. Do you
know all they say to me?

MARTIN:
No.

CAJETAN:
They say: I am a man struggling for certainty, struggling
insanely like a man in a fit, an animal trapped to the
bone with doubt.
    (MARTIN *seems about to have a physical struggle
    with himself.*)

CAJETAN:
Don't you see what could happen out of all this? Men
could be cast out and left to themselves for ever, helpless
and frightened!

MARTIN:
Your eminence, forgive me. I'm tired after my journey—
I think I might faint soon——

CAJETAN:
That's what would become of them without their Mother
Church—with all its imperfections, Peter's rock, without it they'd be helpless and unprotected. Allow them
their sins, their petty indulgences, my son, they're unimportant to the comfort we receive——

MARTIN (*somewhat hysterical*):
Comfort! It—doesn't concern me!

CAJETAN:
We live in thick darkness, and it grows thicker. How will

men find God if they are left to themselves each man
abandoned and only known to himself?

MARTIN:
They'll have to try.

CAJETAN:
I beg of you, my son, I beg of you. Retract.
        (*Pause*)

MARTIN:
Most holy father, I cannot.
        (*Pause*)

CAJETAN:
You look ill. You had better go and rest. (*Pause*) Naturally, you will be released from your order.

MARTIN:
I——

CAJETAN:
Yes?

MARTIN:
As you say, your eminence. Will you refer this matter to
the Pope for his decision?

CAJETAN:
Assuredly. Send in Tetzel.
        (MARTIN *prostrates himself, and then kneels.*
        CAJETAN *is distressed but in control.*)
You know, a time will come when a man will no longer
be able to say, "I speak Latin and am a Christian" and go
his way in peace. There will come frontiers, frontiers of all
kinds—between men—and there'll be no end to them.
        (MARTIN *rises and goes out.* TETZEL *returns.*)

TETZEL:
Yes?

CAJETAN:
No, of course he didn't—that man hates himself. And if he goes to the stake, Tetzel, you can have the pleasure of inscribing it: he could only love others.

(*End of Act Two—Scene Four*)

ACT TWO

SCENE FIVE

A hunting lodge at Magliana in Northern Italy, 1519. Suspended the arms, the brass balls, of the Medici. KARL VON MILTITZ, *a young Chamberlain of the Pope's household is waiting. There are cries off, and sounds of excitement.* POPE LEO THE TENTH *enters with a* HUNTSMAN, *dogs and* DOMINICANS. *He is richly dressed in hunting clothes and long boots. He is indolent, cultured, intelligent, extremely restless, and well able to assimilate the essence of anything before anyone else. While he is listening, he is able to play with a live bird with apparent distraction. Or shoot at a board with a crossbow. Or generally fidget.* MILTITZ *kneels to kiss his toe.*

LEO:
I should forget it. I've got my boots on. Well? Get on with it. We're missing the good weather.

(*He sits and becomes immediately absorbed in his own play, as it seems.* MILTITZ *has a letter, which he reads.*)

MILTITZ:
"To the most blessed father Leo the Tenth, sovereign bishop, Martin Luther, Augustine friar, wishes eternal salvation. I am told that there are vicious reports circulating about me, and that my name is in bad odour with your holiness. I am called a heretic, apostate, traitor and many other insulting names. I cannot understand all this hostility, and I am alarmed by it. But the only basis of my tranquillity remains, as always, a pure and peaceful conscience. Deign to listen to me, most holy father, to me who is like a child.

(LEO *snorts abstractedly.*)

"There have always been, as long as I can remember,
complaints and grumbling in the taverns about the
avarice of the priests and attacks on the power of the
keys. And this has been happening throughout Germany.
When I listened to these things my zeal was aroused for
the glory of Christ, so I warned not one, but several
princes of the Church. But, either they laughed in my
face or ignored me. The terror of your name was too much
for everyone. It was then I published my disputation,
nailing it on the door of the Castle Church here in Wittenberg. And now, most holy father, the whole world has
gone up in flames. Tell me what I should do? I cannot retract; but this thing has drawn down hatred on me from
all sides, and I don't know where to turn to but to you. I
am far too insignificant to appear before the world in a
matter as great as this.

(LEO *snaps his fingers to glance at this passage in
the letter. He does so and returns it to* MILTITZ *who
continues reading.*)

"But in order to quieten my enemies and satisfy my
friends I am now addressing myself to you most holy
father and speak my mind in the greater safety of the
shadow of your wings. All this respect I show to the
power of the keys. If I had not behaved properly it would
have been impossible for the most serene Lord Frederick,
Duke and Elector of Saxony, who shines in your apostolic
favour, to have endured me in his University of Wittenberg. Not if I am as dangerous as is made out by my
enemies. For this reason, most holy father, I fall at the
feet of your holiness, and submit myself to you, with all
I have and all that I am. Declare me right or wrong. Take
my life, or give it back to me, as you please. I shall acknowledge your voice as the voice of Jesus Christ. If I
deserve death, I shall not refuse to die. The earth is God's
and all within it. May He be praised through all eternity,
and may He uphold you for ever. Amen. Written the
day of the Holy Trinity in the year 1518, Martin Luther,
Augustine Friar."

(*They wait for* LEO *to finish his playing and give*

them his full attention. Presently, he gets up and
takes the letter from MILTITZ. *He thinks.*)

LEO:
Double faced German bastard! Why can't he say what
he means? What else?

MILTITZ:
He's said he's willing to be judged by any of the universities of Germany, with the exception of Leipzig, Erfurt
and Frankfurt, which he says are not impartial. He
says it's impossible for him to appear in Rome in person.

LEO:
I'm sure.

MILTITZ:
Because his health wouldn't stand up to the rigours of
the journey.

LEO:
Cunning! Cunning German bastard! What does Staupitz
say for him?

MILTITZ (*reading hastily from another letter*):
"The reverend father, Martin Luther, is the noblest and
most distinguished member of our university. For many
years, we have watched his talents———"

LEO:
Yes, well we know all about that. Write to Cajetan.
Take this down. We charge you to summon before you
Martin Luther. Invoke for this purpose, the aid of our
very dear son in Christ, Maximilian, and all the other
princes in Germany, together with all communities, universities, potentates ecclesiastic and secular. And, once
you get possession of him, keep him in safe custody, so
that he can be brought before us. If, however, he should
return to his duty of his own accord and begs forgiveness, we give you the power to receive him into the perfect unity of our Holy Mother the Church. But, should he

persist in his obstinacy and you cannot secure him, we
authorize you to outlaw him in every part of Germany. To
banish and excommunicate him. As well as all prelates,
religious orders, universities, counts, and dukes who do
not assist in apprehending him. As for the laymen, if
they do not immediately obey your orders, declare them
infamous, deprived of Christian burial and stripped of
anything they may hold either from the apostolic see or
from any lord whatsoever. There's a wild pig in our vine-
yard, and it must be hunted down and shot. Given under
the seal of the Fisherman's Ring, etcetera. That's all.

HE *turns quickly and goes out.*)

(*End of Act Two—Scene Five*)

ACT TWO

SCENE SIX

The Elster Gate, Wittenberg. 1520. Evening. A single bell. As a backcloth the bull issued against Luther. Above it a fish-head and bones. The bull is slashed with the reflection of the flames rising round the Elster Gate where the books of canon law, the papal decretals, are burning furiously. MONKS *come to and fro with more books and documents, and hurl them on the fire.* MARTIN *enters and ascends the pulpit.*

MARTIN:
I have been served with a piece of paper. Let me tell you about it. It has come to me from a latrine called Rome, the capital of the devil's own sweet empire. It is called the papal bull and it claims to excommunicate me, Dr. Martin Luther. These lies they rise up from paper like fumes from the bog of Europe; because papal decretals are the devil's excretals. I'll hold it up for you to see properly. You see the signature? Signed beneath the seal of the Fisherman's Ring by one certain midden cock called Leo, an over-indulged jakes' attendant to Satan himself, a glittering worm in excrement, known to you as his holiness the Pope. You may know him as the head of the Church. Which he may still be: like a fish is the head of a cat's dinner; eyes without sight clutched to a stick of sucked bones. God has told me: there can be no dealings between this cat's dinner and me. And, as for this bull, it's going to roast, it's going to roast and so are the balls of the Medici!

(He descends and casts the bull into the flames. He begins to shake, as if he were unable to breathe; as if he were about to have another fit. Shaking, he kneels.)

97

Oh, God! Oh, God! Oh, thou my God, my God, help
me against the reason and wisdom of the world. You
must—there's only you—to do it. Breathe into me.
Breathe into me, like a lion into the mouth of a stillborn
cub. This cause is not mine but yours. For myself, I've
no business to be dealing with the great lords of this
world. I want to be still, in peace, and alone. Breathe into
me, Jesus. I rely on no man, only on you. My God, my
God do you hear me? Are you dead? Are you dead? No,
you can't die, you can only hide yourself, can't you? Lord,
I'm afraid. I am a child, the lost body of a child. I am
stillborn. Breathe into me, in the name of Thy Son, Jesus
Christ, who shall be my protector and defender, yes, my
mighty fortress, breathe into me. Give me life, oh Lord.
Give me life.

(MARTIN *prays as the deep red light of the flames
flood the darkness around him.*)

(*End of Act Two*)

ACT THREE

Scene One

The Diet of Worms, April 18th, 1521. A gold front-cloth, and on it, in the brightest sunshine of colour, a bold, joyful representation of this unique gathering of princes, electors, dukes, ambassadors, bishops, counts, barons, etc. Perhaps Luther's two-wheeled wagon which brought him to Worms. The mediæval world dressed up for the Renaissance.

Devoid of depth, such scenes are stamped on a brilliant ground of gold. Movement is frozen, recession in space ignored and perspective served by the arrangement of figures, or scenes, one above the other. In this way, landscape is dramatically substituted by objects in layers. The alternative is to do the opposite, in the manner of, say, Altdorfer. Well in front of the cloth is a small rostrum with brass rails sufficient to support one man. If possible, it would be preferable to have this part of the apron projected a little into the audience. Anyway, the aim is to achieve the maximum in physical enlargement of the action, in the sense of physical participation in the theatre, as if everyone watching had their chins resting on the sides of a boxing-ring. Also on the apron, well to the front are several chairs. On one side is a table with about twenty books on it. The table and books may also be represented on the gold cloth. The rostrum has a small crescent of chairs round it. From all corners of the auditorium comes a fanfare of massed trumpets, and, approaching preferably from the auditorium up steps to the apron, come a few members of the Diet audience (who may also be represented on the gold cloth). Preceded by a HERALD, *and seating themselves on the chairs, they should include* THE EMPEROR CHARLES THE FIFTH *(in front of the rostrum),* ALEANDER, THE PAPAL

99

NUNCIO; ULRICH VON HUTTEN, KNIGHT; THE ARCHBISHOP
OF TRIER *and* HIS SECRETARY, JOHAN VON ECK, *who sit
at the table with the books. The trumpets cease, and
they wait.* MARTIN *appears from the stage, and ascends
the rostrum centre.*

ECK (*rising*):
Martin Luther, you have been brought here by His Imperial Majesty so that you may answer two questions. Do you publicly acknowledge being the author of the books you see here? When I asked you this question yesterday, you agreed immediately that the books were indeed your own. Is that right?
    (MARTIN *nods in agreement.*)
When I asked you the second question, you asked if you might be allowed time in which to consider it. Although such time should have been quite unnecessary for an experienced debater and distinguished doctor of theology like yourself, His Imperial Majesty was graciously pleased to grant your request. Well, you have had your time now, a whole day and a night, and so I will repeat the question to you. You have admitted being the author of these books. Do you mean to defend all these books, or will you retract any of them?
    (ECK *sits.* MARTIN *speaks quietly, conversationally, hardly raising his voice throughout, and with simplicity.*)

MARTIN:
Your serene highness, most illustrious princes and gracious lords, I appear before you by God's mercy, and I beg that you will listen patiently. If, through my ignorance, I have not given anyone his proper title or offended in any way against the etiquette of such a place as this, I ask your pardon in advance for a man who finds it hard to know his way outside the few steps from wall to wall of a monk's cell. We have agreed these books are all mine, and they have all been published rightly in my name. I will reply to your second question. I ask your serene majesty and your gracious lordships to take note that not all my books are of the same kind. For instance,

in the first group, I have dealt quite simply with the
values of faith and morality, and even my enemies have
agreed that all this is quite harmless, and can be read
without damaging the most fragile Christian. Even the bull
against me, harsh and cruel as it is, admits that some of
my books are offensive to no one. Perhaps it's the strange
nature of such a questionable compliment, that the bull
goes on to condemn these with the rest, which it con-
siders offensive. If I'm to begin withdrawing these books,
what should I be doing? I should be condemning those
very things my friends and enemies are agreed on. There
is a second group of books I have written, and these all
attack the power of the keys, which has ravaged Christendom. No one can deny this, the evidence is everywhere
and everyone complains of it. And no one has suffered
more from this tyranny than the Germans. They have
been plundered without mercy. If I were to retract those
books now, I should be issuing a licence for more tyranny,
and it is too much to ask of me.

I have also written a third kind of book against certain, private, distinguished, and, apparently—highly established—individuals. They are all defenders of Rome
and enemies of my religion. In these books, it's possible
that I have been more violent than may seem necessary, or,
shall I say, tasteful in one who is, after all, a monk.
But then, I have never set out to be a saint and I've
not been defending my own life, but the teaching of
Christ. So you see, again I'm not free to retract, for if I
did, the present situation would certainly go on just as
before. However, because I am a man and not God, the
only way for me to defend what I have written is to employ the same method used by my Saviour. When He was
being questioned by Annas, the high priest, about His
teaching, and He had been struck in the face by one of
the servants, He replied: "If I have spoken lies tell me
what the lie is." If the Lord Jesus Himself, who could not
err, was willing to listen to the arguments of a servant,
how can I refuse to do the same? Therefore, what I ask,
by the Mercy of God, is let someone expose my errors in
the light of the Gospels. The moment you have done this,

I shall ask you to let me be the first to pick up my books and hurl them in the fire.

I think this is a clear answer to your question. I think I understand the danger of my position well enough. You have made it very clear to me. But I can still think of nothing better than the Word of God being the cause of all the dissension among us. For Christ said, "I have not come to bring peace, but a sword. I have come to set a man against his father." We also have to be sure that the reign of this noble, young Prince Charles, so full of promise, should not end in the misery of Europe. We must fear God alone. I commend myself to your most serene majesty and to your lordships, and humbly pray that you will not condemn me as your enemy. That is all.

ECK (*rising*):
Martin, you have not answered the question put to you. Even if it were true that some of your books are innocuous —a point which, incidentally, we don't concede—we still ask that you cut out these passages which are blasphemous; that you cut out the heresies or whatever could be construed as heresy, and, in fact, that you delete any passage which might be considered hurtful to the Catholic faith. His sacred and imperial majesty is more than prepared to be lenient, and, if you will do these things, he will use his influence with the supreme pontiff to see that the good things in your work are not thrown out with the bad. If, however, you persist in your attitude, there can be no question that all memory of you will be blotted out, and everything you have written, right or wrong, will be forgotten.

You see, Martin, you return to the same place as all other heretics—to Holy Scripture. You demand to be contradicted from Scripture. We can only believe that you must be ill or mad. Do reasons have to be given to anyone who cares to ask a question? Any question? Why, if anyone who questioned the common understanding of the Church on any matter he liked to raise, and had to be answered irrefutably from the Scriptures, there would be nothing certain or decided in Christendom. What would the Jews and Turks and Saracens say if they heard us *debating* whether what we have always believed is true or not? I beg you, Martin, not to believe that you, and you alone, understand the meaning of the Gospels. Don't rate your own opinion so highly, so far beyond that of many other sincere and eminent men. I ask you: don't throw doubt on the most holy, orthodox faith, the faith founded by the most perfect legislator known to us, and spread by His apostles throughout the world, with their blood and miracles. This faith has been defined by sacred councils, and confirmed by the Church. It is your heritage, and we are forbidden to dispute it by the laws of the emperor and the pontiff. Since no amount of argument can lead to a final conclusion, they can only condemn those who refuse to submit to them. The penalties are provided and will be executed. I must, therefore, ask again, I must demand that you answer sincerely, frankly and unambiguously, yes or no: will you or will you not retract your books and the errors contained in them.

MARTIN:
Since your serene majesty and your lordships demand a simple answer, you shall have it, without horns and without teeth. Unless I am shown by the testimony of the Scriptures—for I don't believe in popes or councils—unless I am refuted by Scripture and my conscience is captured by God's own word, I cannot and will not recant, since to act against one's conscience is neither safe nor honest. Here I stand; God help me; I can do no more. Amen.

(*End of Act Three—Scene One*)

ACT THREE

Scene Two

Wittenberg. 1525. A marching hymn, the sound of cannon and shouts of mutilated men. Smoke, a shattered banner bearing the cross and wooden shoe of the Bundschuh, emblem of the Peasants' Movement. A small chapel altar at one side of the stage opposite the pulpit. Centre is a small handcart, and beside it lies the bloody bulk of a peasant's corpse. Downstage stands THE KNIGHT, *fatigued, despondent, stained and dirty.*

KNIGHT:
There was excitement that day. In Worms—that day I mean. Oh, I don't mean now, not now. A lot's happened since then. There's no excitement like that any more. Not unless murder's your idea of excitement. I tell you, you can't have ever known the kind of thrill that monk set off amongst that collection of all kinds of men gathered together there—those few years ago. We all felt it, every one of us, just without any exception, you couldn't help it, even if you didn't want to, and, believe me, most of those people didn't want to. His scalp looked blotchy and itchy, and you felt sure, just looking at him, his body must be permanently sour and white all over, even whiter than his face and like a millstone to touch. He'd sweated so much by the time he'd finished, I could smell every inch of him even from where I was. But he fizzed like a hot spark in a trail of gunpowder going off in us, that dowdy monk, he went off in us, and nothing could stop it, and it blew up and there was nothing we could do, any of us, that was it. I just felt quite sure, quite certain in my own mind nothing could ever be the same again, just simply that. Something had taken place, something had changed and become something

104

else, an event had occurred in the flesh, in the flesh and
the breath—like, even like when the weight of that body
slumped on its wooden crotchpiece and the earth grew
dark. That's the kind of thing I mean by happen, and this
also happened in very likely the same manner to all those
of us who stood there, friends and enemies alike. I don't
think, no I don't think even if I could speak and write
like him, I could begin to give you an idea of what we
thought, or what some of us thought, of what we might
come to. Obviously, we couldn't have all felt quite the
same way, but I wanted to burst my ears with shouting
and draw my sword, no, not draw it, I wanted to pluck
it as if it were a flower in my blood and plunge it into
whatever he would have told me to.

(THE KNIGHT *is lost in his own thoughts, then his
eyes catch the body of the peasant. He takes a swipe
at the cart.*)

If one could only understand him. He baffles me, I just
can't make him out. Anyway, it never worked out. (*To
corpse*) Did it, my friend? Not the way we expected anyway, certainly not the way *you* expected, but who'd have
ever thought we might end up on different sides, him on
one and us on the other. That when the war came between you and them, he'd be there beating the drum for
them outside the slaughter house, and beating it louder
and better than anyone, hollering for *your* blood, cutting
you up in your thousands, and hanging you up to drip
away into the fire for good. Oh well, I suppose all those
various groups were out for their different things, or the
same thing really, all out for what we could get, and more
than any of us had the right to expect. They were all
the same, all those big princes and archbishops, the cut
rate nobility and rich layabouts, honourable this and
thats scrabbling like boars round a swill bucket for every
penny those poor peasants never had. All those great
abbots with their dewlaps dropped and hanging on their
necks like goose's eggs, and then those left-over knights,
like me for instance, I suppose, left-over men, impover-
ished, who'd seen better days and were scared and'd
stick at nothing to try and make sure they couldn't get
any worse. Yes. . . . Not one of them could read the

words WAY OUT when it was written up for them, marked
out clearly and unmistakably in the pain of too many
men. Yes. They say, you know, that the profit motive—
and I'm sure you know all about that one—they say that
the profit motive was born with the invention of double
entry book-keeping in the monasteries. Book-keeping! In
the monasteries, and ages before any of us had ever got
round to burning them down. But, you know, for men
with such a motive, there is only really one entry. The
profit is theirs, the loss is someone else's, and usually
they don't even bother to write it up.

(*He nudges the corpse with his toe.*)

Well, it was your old loss wasn't it, dead loss, in fact,
my friend, you could say his life was more or less a
write-off right from the day he was born. Wasn't it?
Um? And all the others like him, everywhere, now and
after him.

(THE KNIGHT *starts rather weakly to load the body
on to the cart.* MARTIN *enters, a book in his hands.
They look at each other then* MARTIN *at the* PEAS-
ANT. THE KNIGHT *takes his book and glances at it,
but he doesn't miss* MARTIN *shrink slightly from the
peasant.*)

Another of yours?

(*He hands it back.*)

Do you think it'll sell as well as the others? (*Pause*)
I dare say it will. Someone's always going to listen to
you. No?

(MARTIN *moves to go, but* THE KNIGHT *stops him.*)

Martin. Just a minute.

(*He turns and places his hand carefully, ritually,
on the body in the cart. He smears the blood from it
over* MARTIN.)

There we are. That's better.

(MARTIN *makes to move again, but again* THE
KNIGHT *stops him.*)

You're all ready now. You even look like a butcher——

MARTIN:
God is the butcher——

KNIGHT:
Don't you?

MARTIN:
Why don't you address your abuse to Him?

KNIGHT:
Never mind—you're wearing His apron.
        (MARTIN *moves to the stairs of the pulpit.*)
It suits you. (*Pause*) Doesn't it? (*Pause*) That day in
Worms (*pause*) you were like a pig under glass weren't
you? Do you remember it? I could smell every inch of
you even where I was standing. All you've ever managed
to do is convert everything into stench and dying and
peril, but you could have done it, Martin, and you were
the only one who could have ever done it. You could
even have brought freedom and order in at one and the
same time.

MARTIN:
There's no such thing as an orderly revolution. Anyway,
Christians are called to suffer, not fight.

KNIGHT:
But weren't we all of us, all of us, without any excep-
tions to please any old interested parties, weren't we all
redeemed by Christ's blood? (*Pointing to the peasant*)
Wasn't he included when the Scriptures were being dic-
tated? Or was it just you who was made free, you and
the princes you've taken up with, and the rich burghers
and——

MARTIN:
Free? (*Ascends the pulpit steps.*) The princes blame
me, you blame me and the peasants blame me——

KNIGHT (*following up the steps*):
You put the water in the wine didn't you?

MARTIN:
When I see chaos, then I see the devil's organ and then
I'm afraid. Now, that's enough——

KNIGHT:
You're breaking out again——

MARTIN:
Go away——

KNIGHT:
Aren't you?
    (MARTIN *makes a sudden effort to push him back
    down the steps, but* THE KNIGHT *hangs on firmly.*)

MARTIN:
Get back!

KNIGHT:
Aren't you, you're breaking out again, you canting pig,
I can smell you from here!

MARTIN:
He heard the children of Israel, didn t He?

KNIGHT:
Up to the ears in revelation, aren't you?

MARTIN:
And didn't He deliver them out of the Land of Pharaoh?

KNIGHT:
You canting pig, aren't you?

MARTIN:
Well? Didn't He?

KNIGHT:
Cock's wounds! Don't hold your Bible to my head, piggy,
there's enough revelation of my own in there for me, in

what I see for myself from here! (*Taps his forehead.*)
Hold your gospel against that!

(THE KNIGHT *grabs* MARTIN'S *hand and clamps it to
his head.*)

KNIGHT:
You're killing the spirit, and you're killing it with the
letter. You've been swilling about in the wrong place,
Martin, in your own stink and ordure. Go on! You've got
your hand on it, that's all the holy spirit there is, and it's
all you'll ever get so feel it!

(*They struggle, but* THE KNIGHT *is very weak by
now, and* MARTIN *is able to wrench himself away
and up into the pulpit.*)

MARTIN:
The world was conquered by the Word, the Church is
maintained by the Word——

KNIGHT:
Word? What Word? Word? That word, whatever that
means, is probably just another old relic or indulgence,
and you know what you did to those! Why, none of it
might be any more than poetry, have you thought of
that, Martin. Poetry! Martin, you're a poet, there's no
doubt about that in anybody's mind, you're a poet, but do
you know what most men believe in, in their hearts—
because they don't see in images like you do—they believe
in their hearts that Christ was a man as we are, and that
He was a prophet and a teacher, and they also believe in
their hearts that His supper is a plain meal like their
own—if they're lucky enough to get it—a plain meal of
bread and wine! A plain meal with no garnish and no
word. And *you* helped them to begin to believe it!

MARTIN (*pause*):
Leave me.

KNIGHT:
Yes. What's there to stay for? I've been close enough to
you for too long. I even smell like you.

MARTIN (*roaring with pain*):
I smell because of my own argument, I smell because I
never stop disputing with Him, and because I expect Him
to keep His Word. Now then! If your peasant rebelled
against that Word, that was worse than murder because
it laid the whole country waste, and who knows now what
God will make of us Germans!

KNIGHT:
Don't blame God for the Germans, Martin! (*Laughs*)
Don't do that! You thrashed about more than anyone on
the night they were conceived!

MARTIN:
Christ! Hear me! My words pour from Your Body! They
deserved their death, these swarming peasants! They
kicked against authority, they plundered and bargained
and all in Your name! Christ, believe me! (*To* THE
KNIGHT) I demanded it, I prayed for it, and I got it! Take
that lump away! Now, drag it away with you!
            (THE KNIGHT *prepares to trundle off the cart and
            corpse.*)

KNIGHT:
All right, my friend. Stay with your nun then. Marry and
stew with your nun. Most of the others have. Stew with
her, like a shuddering infant in *her* bed. You think you'll
manage?

MARTIN (*lightly*):
At least my father'll praise me for *that*.

KNIGHT:
Your father?
            (THE KNIGHT *shrugs, pushes the cart wearily, and
            goes off.* MARTIN'S *head hangs over the edge of the
            pulpit.*)

MARTIN:
I (*whispering*) trust you. . . . I trust you. . . . You've

overcome the world. . . . I trust you. . . . You're all I
wish to have . . . ever. . . .

> (*Slumped over the pulpit, he seems to be uncon-
> scious. Then he makes an effort to recover, as if
> he had collapsed in the middle of a sermon.*)

I expect you must . . . I'm sure you must remember—
Abraham. Abraham was—he was an old man . . . a . . .
very old man indeed, in fact, he was a hundred years
old, when what was surely, what must have been a
miracle happened, to a man of his years—a son was
born to him. A son. Isaac he called him. And he loved
Isaac. Well, he loved him with such intensity, one can
only diminish it by description. But to Abraham his little
son was a miraculous thing, a small, incessant . . . animal
. . . astonishment. And in the child he sought the father.
But, one day, God said to Abraham: Take your little son
whom you love so much, kill him, and make a sacrifice
of him. And in that moment everything inside Abraham
seemed to shrivel once and for all. Because it had seemed
to him that God had promised him life through his son.
So then he took the boy and prepared to kill him, strap-
ping him down to the wood of the burnt offering just as
he had been told to do. And he spoke softly to the boy,
and raised the knife over his little naked body, the boy
struggling not to flinch or blink his eyes. Never, save
in Christ, was there such obedience as in that moment,
and, if God had blinked, the boy would have died then,
but the Angel intervened, and the boy was released, and
Abraham took him up in his arms again. In the teeth of
life we seem to die, but God says no—in the teeth of
death we live. If He butchers us, He makes us live.

> (*Enter* THE KNIGHT, *who stands watching him, the
> Bundschuh banner in his hands.*)

Heart of my Jesus save me; Heart of my Saviour deliver
me; Heart of my Shepherd guard me; Heart of my Master
teach me; Heart of my King govern me; Heart of my
Friend stay with me.

> (*Enter* KATHERINE VON BORA, *his bride, accom-
> panied by two* MONKS. MARTIN *rises from the pulpit
> and goes towards her. A simple tune is played on a
> simple instrument. She takes his hand, and they kneel*

together centre. THE KNIGHT *watches. Then he smashes the banner he has been holding, and tosses the remains onto the altar.)*

(End of Act Three—Scene Two)

ACT THREE

Scene Three

A hymn. The Eremite Cloister. Wittenberg. 1530. The refectory table, and on it two places set, and the remains of two meals. MARTIN *is seated alone. The vigour of a man in his late thirties, and at the height of his powers, has settled into the tired pain of a middle age struggling to rediscover strength.*

KATHERINE *enters with a jug of wine. She is a big, pleasant-looking girl, almost thirty.*

MARTIN:
How is he?

KATHERINE:
He's all right. He's just coming. Wouldn't let me help him. I think he's been sick.

MARTIN:
Poor old chap. After living all your life in a monastery, one's stomach doesn't take too easily to your kind of cooking.

KATHERINE:
Wasn't it all right?

MARTIN:
Oh, it was fine, just too much for an old monk's shrivelled digestion to chew on, that's all.

KATHERINE:
Oh, I see. *You're* all right, aren't you?

113

MARTIN:

Yes, I'm all right, thank you, my dear. (*Smile*) I expect
I'll suffer later though.

KATHERINE:

You like your food, so don't make out you don't.

MARTIN:

Well, I prefer it to fasting. Did you never hear the story
of the soldier who was fighting in the Holy Crusades? No?
Well, he was told by his officer that if he died in battle,
he would dine in Paradise with Christ; and the soldier
ran away. When he came back after the battle, they
asked him why he'd run away. "Didn't you want to dine
with Christ?" they said. And he replied, "No, I'm fasting
today."

KATHERINE:

I've brought you some more wine.

MARTIN:

Thank you.

KATHERINE:

Should help you to sleep.
    (STAUPITZ *enters, supporting himself with a stick.*)

MARTIN:

There you are! I thought you'd fallen down the jakes
—right into the devil's loving arms.

STAUPITZ:

I'm so sorry. I was—I was wandering about a bit.

MARTIN:

Well, come and sit down. Katie's brought us some more
wine.

STAUPITZ:

I can't get over being here again. It's so odd. This place

was full of men. And now, now there's only you, you
and Katie. It's very, very strange.

KATHERINE:
I shouldn't stay up too long, Martin. You didn't sleep well
again last night. I could hear you—hardly breathing all
night.

MARTIN (*amused*):
You could hear me hardly breathing?

KATHERINE:
You know what I mean. When you don't sleep, it keeps
me awake too. Good night, Dr. Staupitz.

STAUPITZ:
Good night, my dear. Thank you for the dinner. It was ex-
cellent. I'm so sorry I wasn't able to do justice to it.

KATHERINE:
That's all right. Martin's always having the same kind of
trouble.

STAUPITZ:
Yes? Well, he's not changed much then.

MARTIN:
Not a bit. Even Katie hasn't managed to shift my bowels
for me, have you?

KATHERINE:
And if it's not that, he can't sleep.

MARTIN:
Yes, Katie, you've said that already. I've also got gout,
piles and bells in my ears. Dr. Staupitz has had to put up
with all my complaints for longer than you have, isn't
that right?

KATHERINE:
Well, try not to forget what I said. (*She kisses* MARTIN's *cheeks.*)

MARTIN:
Good night, Katie.
(*She goes out.*)

STAUPITZ:
Well, *you've* never been so well looked after.

MARTIN:
It's a shame everyone can't marry a nun. They're fine cooks, thrifty housekeepers, and splendid mothers. Seems to me there are three ways out of despair. One is faith in Christ, the second is to become enraged by the world and make its nose bleed for it, and the third is the love of a woman. Mind you, they don't all necessarily work—at least, only part of the time. Sometimes, I'm lying awake in the devil's own sweat, and I turn to Katie and touch her. And I say: get me out, Katie, please, Katie, please try and get me out. And sometimes, sometimes she actually drags me out. Poor old Katie, fishing about there in bed with her great, hefty arms, trying to haul me out.

STAUPITZ:
She's good.

MARTIN:
Wine?

STAUPITZ:
Not much. I must go to bed myself.

MARTIN:
Help you sleep. You're looking tired.

STAUPITZ:
Old. Our old pear tree's in blossom, I see. You've looked after it.

MARTIN:
I like to get in a bit in the garden, if I can. I like to think
it heals my bones somehow. Anyway, I always feel a bit
more pleased with myself afterwards.

STAUPITZ:
We'd a few talks under that tree.

MARTIN:
Yes.

STAUPITZ:
Martin, it's so still. I don't think I'd ever realized how
eloquent a monk's silence really was. It was a voice.
(*Pause*) It's gone. (*He shakes his head, pause.*) How's
your father these days?

MARTIN:
Getting old too, but he's well enough.

STAUPITZ:
Is he—is he pleased with you?

MARTIN:
He was never pleased about anything I ever did. Not when
I took my master's degree or when I got to be Dr.
Luther. Only when Katie and I were married and she
got pregnant. Then he was pleased.

STAUPITZ:
Do you remember Brother Weinand?

MARTIN:
I ought to. He used to hold my head between my knees
when I felt faint in the choir.

STAUPITZ:
I wonder what happened to him. (*Pause*) He had the
most beautiful singing voice.

MARTIN:

My old friend, you're unhappy. I'm sorry. (*Pause*) We monks were really no good to anyone, least of all to ourselves, every one of us rolled up like a louse in the Almighty's overcoat.

STAUPITZ:

Yes. Well, you always have a way of putting it. I was always having to give you little lectures about the fanatic way you'd observe the Rule all the time.

MARTIN:

Yes, and you talked me out of it, remember? (*Pause*) Father, are *you* pleased with me?

STAUPITZ:

Pleased with you? My dear son, I'm not anyone or anything to be pleased with you any more. When we used to talk together underneath that tree you were like a child.

MARTIN:

A child.

STAUPITZ:

Manhood was something you had to be flung into, my son. You dangled your toe in it longer than most of us could ever bear. But you're not a frightened little monk any more who's come to his prior for praise or blame. Every time you belch now, the world stops what it's doing and listens. Do you know, when I first came to take over this convent, there weren't thirty books published every year. And now, last year it was more like six or seven hundred, and most of those published in Wittenberg too.

MARTIN:

The best turn God ever did Himself was giving us a printing press. Sometimes I wonder what He'd have done without it.

STAUPITZ:

I heard the other day they're saying the world's going to end in 1532.

MARTIN:

It sounds as good a date as any other. Yes—1532. That
could easily be the end of the world. You could write a
book about it, and just call it that—1532.

STAUPITZ:

I'm sorry, Martin. I didn't mean to come and see you
after all this time and start criticizing. Forgive me, I'm
getting old and a bit silly and frightened, that meal was
just too much for me. It wasn't that I didn't——

MARTIN:

Please—I'm sorry too. Don't upset yourself. I'm used to
critics, John. They just help you to keep your muscles
from getting slack. All those hollow cavillers, that subtle
clown Erasmus, for instance. He ought to know better,
but all he wants to do is to be able to walk on eggs without breaking any. As for that mandrill-arsed English ba-
boon Henry, that leprous son of a bitch never had an
idea of his own to jangle on a tombstone, let alone call
himself Defender of the Faith.
   (*Pause.* STAUPITZ *hasn't responded to his attempt at
   lightness.*)
Still, one thing for Erasmus, he didn't fool about with all
the usual cant and rubbish about indulgences and the
Pope and Purgatory. No, he went right to the core of it.
He's still up to his ears with stuff about morality, and
men being able to save themselves. No one does good,
not anyone. God is true and one. But, and this is what he
can't grasp, He's utterly incomprehensible and beyond
the reach of minds. A man's will is like a horse standing
between two riders. If God jumps on its back, it'll go
where God wants it to. But if Satan gets up there, it'll go
where he leads it. And not only that, the horse can't
choose its rider. That's left up to them, to those two.
(*Pause*) Why are you accusing me? What have I done?

STAUPITZ:

I'm not accusing you, Martin. You know that. A just
man is his own accuser. Because a just man judges as he
is.

MARTIN:
What's that mean? I'm not just?

STAUPITZ:
You try. What else can you do?

MARTIN:
You mean those damned peasants, don't you? You think
I should have encouraged them!

STAUPITZ:
I don't say that.

MARTIN:
Well, what do you say?

STAUPITZ:
You needn't have encouraged the princes. They were
butchered and *you* got them to do it. And they had just
cause, Martin. They did, didn't they?

MARTIN:
I didn't say they hadn't.

STAUPITZ:
Well, then?

MARTIN:
Do you remember saying to me, "Remember, brother, you
started this in the name of the Lord Jesus Christ"?

STAUPITZ:
Well?

MARTIN:
Father, the world can't be ruled with a rosary. They were
a mob, a mob, and if they hadn't been held down and
slaughtered, there'd have been a thousand more tyrants
instead of half a dozen. It was a mob, and because it
was a mob it was against Christ. No man can die for another, or believe for another or answer for another. The

moment they try they become a mob. If we're lucky we can be persuaded in our own mind, and the most we can hope for is to die each one for himself. Do I have to tell you what Paul says? You read! "Let every soul be subject unto the highest powers. For there is no power but of God: the powers that be are ordained of God. Whosoever therefore resisteth that power, resisteth the ordinance of God": that's Paul, Father, and that's Scripture! "And they that resist shall receive to themselves damnation."

STAUPITZ:
Yes, you're probably right.

MARTIN:
"Love worketh no ill to his neighbour: therefore love is the fulfilling of the law."

STAUPITZ:
Yes, well it seems to be all worked out. I must be tired.

MARTIN:
It was worked out for me.

STAUPITZ:
I'd better get off to bed.

MARTIN:
They're trying to turn me into a fixed star, Father, but I'm a shifting planet. You're leaving me.

STAUPITZ:
I'm not leaving you, Martin. I love you. I love you as much as any man has ever loved most women. But we're not two protected monks chattering under a pear tree in a garden any longer. The world's changed. For one thing, you've made a thing called Germany; you've unlaced a language and taught it to the Germans, and the rest of the world will just have to get used to the sound of it. As we once made the body of Christ from bread, you've made the body of Europe, and whatever

our pains turn out to be, they'll attack the rest of the
world too. You've taken Christ away from the low mum-
blings and soft voices and jewelled gowns and the tiaras
and put Him back where He belongs. In each man's soul.
We owe so much to you. All I beg of you is not to be
too violent. In spite of everything, of everything you've
said and shown us, there *were* men, *some* men who did
live holy lives here once. Don't—don't believe you, only
you are right.

> (STAUPITZ *is close to tears, and* MARTIN *doesn't
> know what to do.*)

MARTIN:
What else can I do? What can I do?
> (*He clutches at his abdomen.*)

STAUPITZ:
What is it?

MARTIN:
Oh, the old trouble, that's all. That's all.

STAUPITZ:
Something that's puzzled me, and I've always meant to
ask you.

MARTIN:
Well?

STAUPITZ:
When you were before the Diet in Worms, and they
asked you those two questions—why did you ask for that
extra day to think over your reply?

MARTIN:
Why?

STAUPITZ:
You'd known what your answer was going to be for
months. Heaven knows, you told me enough times. Why
did you wait?
> (*Pause*)

MARTIN:
I wasn't certain.

STAUPITZ:
And were you? Afterwards?

MARTIN:
I listened for God's voice, but all I could hear was my own.

STAUPITZ:
Were you sure?
(*Pause*)

MARTIN:
No.
(STAUPITZ *kisses him.*)

STAUPITZ:
Thank you, my son. May God bless you. I hope you sleep better. Goodnight.

MARTIN:
Goodnight, Father.
(STAUPITZ *goes out, and* MARTIN *is left alone. He drinks his wine.*)

MARTIN:
Oh, Lord, I believe. I believe. I do believe. Only help my unbelief.
(*He sits slumped in his chair.* KATHERINE *enters. She is wearing a nightdress, and carries in her arms* HANS, *their young son.*)

KATHERINE:
He was crying out in his sleep. Must have been dreaming again. Aren't you coming to bed?

MARTIN:
Shan't be long, Katie. Shan't be long.

KATHERINE:
All right, but try not to be too long. You look—well,
you don't look as well as you should.
    (*She turns to go.*)

MARTIN:
Give him to me.

KATHERINE:
What?

MARTIN:
Give him to me.

KATHERINE:
What do you mean, what for? He'll get cold down here.

MARTIN:
No, he won't. Please, Katie. Let me have him.

KATHERINE:
You're a funny man. All right, but only for five minutes. Don't just sit there all night. He's gone back to sleep
now. He'll be having another dream if you keep him
down here.

MARTIN:
Thank you, Katie.

KATHERINE:
There! Keep him warm now! He's *your* son.

MARTIN:
I will. Don't worry.

KATHERINE:
Well, make sure you do. (*Pausing on way out*) Don't be
long now, Martin.

MARTIN:
Goodnight, Kate.

(*She goes out, leaving* MARTIN *with the sleeping child in his arms.*)

MARTIN (*softly*):
What was the matter? Was it the devil bothering you? Um? Was he? Old nick? Up you, old nick. Well, don't worry. One day you might even be glad of him. So long as you can show him your little backside. That's right, show him your backside and let him have it. So try not to be afraid. The dark isn't quite as thick as all that. You know, my father had a son, and he'd to learn a hard lesson, which is a human being is a helpless little animal, but he's not created by his father, but by God. It's hard to accept you're anyone's son, and you're not the father of yourself. So, don't have dreams so soon, my son. *They'll* be having *you* soon enough.
(*He gets up.*)
You should have seen me at Worms. I was almost like you that day, as if I'd learned to play again, to play, to play out in the world, like a naked child. "I have come to set a man against his father," I said, and they listened to me. Just like a child. Sh! We must go to bed, mustn't we? A little while, and you *shall* see me. Christ said that, my son. I hope that'll be the way of it again. I hope so. Let's just hope so, eh? Eh? Let's just hope so.

(MARTIN *holds the child in his arms, and then walks off slowly*).

The End.